Education Policy

Education Policy

Bridging the Divide Between Theory and Practice

Second Edition

JEROME G. DELANEY

17 18 19 20 21 5 4 3 2 1

Printed and manufactured in Canada

Brush Education Inc.
www.brusheducation.ca
contact@brusheducation.ca

Editorial: Leslie Vermeer, Shauna Babiuk

Cover Design: Dean Pickup; Cover Images: books: Marekidowski, Dreamstime: chalkboard: Ganna Todica, Dreamstime

Interior Design and Layout: Carol Dragich, Dragich Design

Library and Archives Canada Cataloguing in Publication

Delaney, Jerome G.
[Educational policy studies]
    Education policy : bridging the divide between theory and practice
/ Jerome G. Delaney. -- Second edition.

Previously published under title: Educational policy studies.
Includes bibliographical references and index.
Issued in print and electronic formats.
ISBN 978-1-55059-724-0 (softcover).--ISBN 978-1-55059-725-7 (PDF).--
ISBN 978-1-55059-726-4 (Kindle).--ISBN 978-1-55059-727-1 (EPUB)

    1. Education and state. 2. Textbooks. I. Title. II. Title: Educational
policy studies.

LC71.D44 2017   379   C2017-906353-7
                                                        C2017-906354-5

We acknowledge the support of the Government of Canada
Nous reconnaissons l'appui du gouvernement du Canada | Canada

Dedication
To Stacey, Lindsay and Colin

Contents

Acknowledgements ix

Preface x

1 An Overview of Education Policy 1

2 Values and Principles in Education Policy 7

3 Types of Education Policies 14

4 Policy Analysis 24

5 Policy Development 36

6 Policy Implementation 42

7 Policy Evaluation 52

8 Policy Dissemination 59

9 Policy and Regulations 62

10 The Role of Research in Policy-Making 67

11 Issues and Concerns in Policy Development 73

12 Policy and Education Reform 84

13 A Research Study on Education Policy 89

14 The Future of Education Policy 93

15 Concluding Thoughts 98

References 101

About the Author 106

Subject and Name Index 107

Acknowledgements

The writing of the second edition of this book on education policy has been a wonderful exercise, more so than the original edition for a variety of reasons. The first edition was penned when I was a full-time high school principal, which brought with it a number of challenges related to time. The second edition was written while I was a full-time academic; time was still an issue but more manageable than in my previous position.

There are a number of individuals whom I wish to thank for this new edition:

1. my students, both undergraduate and graduate, over these past several years who gave me the opportunity to discuss my thoughts and research findings with them. Their comments from a practitioner's perspective were a great help in allowing me to expand and refine my thinking about education policy.
2. Ms. Lauri Seidlitz, managing editor at Brush Education, who initially saw the value of this second edition and decided to take on this project. She was always delightful and an absolute pleasure to work with; thank you, Lauri, for seeing this second edition come to fruition.
3. my editor, Dr. Leslie Vermeer, who at times challenged me with reference to the various points in the text but who, at all times, was the consummate professional and like Lauri, was always delightful and an absolute pleasure to work with. Because of her exceptional editorial skills, this second edition is, I feel, much stronger academically. A sincere thank you, Leslie, for your expertise, unlimited patience, and friendship during the editing process.

And lastly, to my family—wife Philomena, son Colin, daughters Lindsay (Gino) and Stacey (Richard) and our beautiful granddaughter Olivia for their unwavering support and unlimited patience in my academic pursuits. Hugs and appreciation to all.

Preface

Originally published in 2002 under the title *Education Policy Studies: A Practical Approach*, this book is a second edition under a new title, *Education Policy: Bridging the Divide Between Theory and Practice*. The title was changed to more accurately reflect the book's content.

I hope this book is a primer on all things related to education policy. Most texts on this subject discuss policy from a macro perspective; this text takes more of a micro approach. Specifically, the subject is broken down into a number of manageable subtopics: definition, values and principles, types, policy analysis, policy development, policy implementation, policy evaluation, and the relationship between research and policy.

Other texts assume the reader's knowledge and understanding of these basic concepts, sometimes causing the reader to feel overwhelmed by the material as it deals with the big picture of policy, with only passing reference to specific policy initiatives. The approach taken in this book derives from my work experience in the public school system, which tends to be a pragmatic and realistic setting. I have consciously adopted that approach in this book, and I hope this content will lead the reader and student of education policy to become a little more knowledgeable and a little more understanding of what education policy is all about.

1

An Overview of Education Policy

The word *policy* has become quite common in today's society. We read about public policy, foreign policy, health care policy, board policy, monetary policy, and immigration policy, to mention only a few. Back in 1995, Silver coined the phrase *policy rage*, which he used to describe society's preoccupation with policy. Today, policy has taken on an even more vigorous role in society. Some of that may result from our society's becoming more litigious, meaning that people in general are much more conscious of their legal rights and are less reluctant than ever before to advocate for those rights. In negligence and liability court cases, an institution's policies come under greater scrutiny and can often be instrumental in helping to decide the outcome of specific cases. Although helping to decide outcomes in specific cases is not necessarily the primary purpose of policy, it is indeed a positive by-product of having policies in place.

Education policy is taking on a greater significance in our K–12 school systems, so it is imperative that educators have a working and practical knowledge of what education policy is all about.

Education Policy Studies

What do we mean when we use the term *education policy studies*? Several images come to mind: research centered on the specific subject of the policy; decision-making (ideally) of the shared and collegial kind; the current state of what is happening with that particular subject—the positives and the negatives, and various other related issues and concerns; and what the current research tells us with respect to that subject.

Nagel (1980) suggested that policy studies are concerned with "the nature, causes, and effects of alternative public policies" (p. 391). A less erudite conceptualization of policy studies might point to policy analysis, policy development, policy implementation, policy evaluation, and policy revision. Policy analysis involves studying an issue and consulting with the key stakeholders to determine the "slant" a specific policy should take. The other areas similarly involve the actual development and the related processes of implementing, evaluating, and revising of policy to ensure it achieves its objectives.

There is a certain degree of ambiguity associated with education policy studies. According to Boyd and Plank (1994), "because of the richness and variety of purposes and approaches involved in policy studies, it is not surprising that there is ambiguity about what constitutes the field" (p. 1836). They attribute part of that difficulty to how dramatically the field has changed since its initial growth spurt in the early 1960s.

Wildavsky (1985) concluded that the field has moved from a "macro-macho" approach to a "micro-incremental" approach:

> The origins of the "macro-macho" versions of policy analysis—
> the belief that large national problems, from defense to welfare, are
> susceptible to solution through applications of economic analy-
> sis—were rooted in the intersection between economics, statistics,
> computing, and the defense "think tanks" of the early 1960s. (p. 28)

It was assumed in the 1960s that large-scale economic models could capture the complexity of policy problems and identify the most efficient policy alternatives. Out of this tradition emerged an ambitious and robust paradigm for policy analysis that continues to influence the field today (Boyd & Plank, 1994). Although the macro-macho versions may be of some relevance to education policy today, I contend that a more viable approach to policy analysis in education would be micro-incremental, as people (students, educators, parents, and various other stakeholders) should be at the center of all education policy.

In an effort to decrease that ambiguity—or as some critics might suggest, perhaps to add to that ambiguity—many graduate schools of education have now developed specific courses in education policy studies. I think students pursuing graduate degrees in educational leadership and curriculum studies would be well served by having the opportunity to critically examine the whole area of education policy. The educator—whether a teacher in the classroom, a principal, or a district-level administrator—regularly confronts some aspects of policy in the multitude of decisions he or she makes every day.

Policy Defined

There are as many definitions of education policy as there are writers on the subject. As Cunningham (1963) stated almost six decades ago, "policy is like an elephant—you recognize one when you see it, but it is somewhat more difficult to define" (p. 229), a statement that is still relevant today. Duke and Canady (1991) concluded that a commonly accepted definition of policy is still missing in both the literature and school practice. Definitions range from the very brief to the rather long and convoluted. Here is a sampling for consideration.

Caldwell and Spinks (1988) defined education policy as "a statement of purpose and one or more broad guidelines as to how that purpose is to be achieved, which, taken together, provide a framework for the operation of the school or programme" (p. 41). They further stated that policy may allow discretion in its implementation, with the basis for that discretion often stated as part of the policy.

Sergiovanni, Burlingame, Coombs, and Thurston (1999) referred to policy as "any authoritative communication about how individuals in certain positions should behave under specified conditions" (p. 230). They offered the following illustration:

> The principal who issues a memorandum saying that "no teacher should leave the building before 3:45 p.m. on school days" has fashioned a policy—so has the superintendent who directs principals not to suspend pupils for more than three days without board approval, and the state legislature that enacts a law requiring students to pass a competency test before high school graduation. (p. 230)

First (1992) characterized policy as "a vision of where we want to go and guidelines for getting there" (p. 14). She went on to say,

> it is important that we agree that policy is wide, rather than narrow, long term rather than short term, and that it involves leadership. The leader is needed to paint that vision that becomes the policy statements. (p. 14)

Downey (1988) perceived policy as an instrument of governance and offered two definitions:

> an authoritative determination, by a governing authority, of a society's intents and priorities and an authoritative allocation of resources to those intents and priorities; an authoritative guideline to institutions governed by the authority (and persons who work in them) as to what their intents are to be and how they are to set out to achieve them. (p. 10)

Levin and Young (1994), on the other hand, described policy more broadly as "a general approach to things, intended to guide behavior, and which has broad implications within a particular setting, whether it be a country, province or school" (p. 60). They further stated that

> policies shape the structure of schools, the resources available in schools, the curriculum, the teaching staff, and, to a considerable extent, the round of daily activities. Policies determine how much money is spent, by whom, and on what, how teachers are paid, how students are evaluated, and most other aspects of schools as we know them. The impact of policies can be illustrated by listing just a few areas of education policy. Some important policy areas [include] school consolidation, language policy, and Aboriginal education . . . (pp. 60–61)

Guba (1984) has identified eight distinct concepts of policy, three of which are relevant here:

1. Policy is an assertion of intents and goals.
2. Policy is sanctioned behavior.
3. Policy is a norm of conduct characterized by consistency and regularity in some substantive action area. (p. 65)

One of my favorite definitions of policy is proffered by Marshall and Gerstl-Pepin (2005): "policy then is the result of politics, the result of that allocation of values; policy is what governments choose to do" (p. 5). Fowler (2009) took a broad view of what policy is and defined it as "the dynamic and value-laden process through which a political system handles a public problem. It included a government's expressed intentions and official enactments, as well as its consistent patterns of activity and inactivity" (pp. 3–4).

Despite writers' and researchers' unique perspectives on what they consider policy to be, a number of common elements are inherent in their definitions:

1. Policy is a formalized act.
2. Policy has an agreed-on objective.
3. Policy is approved or sanctioned by an institutional body or authority.
4. Policy provides some kind of standard for measuring performance.

As students of policy, we must keep in mind the points articulated here as we continue to develop our understandings of what policy is about.

Benefits of Policy

The benefits of well-written, well-organized, and regularly updated policies to any educational institution and its members should be obvious. Nonetheless, Caldwell and Spinks (1988) provided the following list of such benefits:

1. Policies demonstrate that the school is being operated in an efficient and business-like manner. When policies are written, there is rarely any ambiguity with regard to the goals of the school and how the school is to be administered.

2. Policies ensure, to a considerable extent, that there will be uniformity and consistency in decisions and in operational procedures. Good policy makes *ad hoc* or whimsical decision-making difficult.

3. Policies must be consistent with those for the system as a whole and with the various statutes that constitute school law. Policies thus add strength to the position of the head teacher and staff when possible legal actions arise.

4. Policies help ensure meetings are orderly. Valuable time will be saved when a new problem can be handled quickly and effectively because of its relationship to an existing policy.

5. Policies foster stability and continuity. Administrators and teachers may come and go, but well-written and constantly updated policies remain. Such policies make clear the general direction of the school and therefore facilitate orientation of newly appointed members of staff of the school, and of the council or governing body, where such a group exists.

6. Policies provide the framework for planning in the school.

7. Policies assist the school in the assessment of the instructional program. Written and publicly disseminated statements of policy show that the policy group is willing to be held accountable for decisions.

8. Policies clarify functions and responsibilities of the policy group, head teacher, and staff. All can work with greater efficiency, satisfaction, and commitment when school policies are well known, understood, and accepted (p. 93).

These benefits are pragmatic in nature and palatable to stakeholders. Policy sometimes runs the risk of being nonpragmatic or esoteric and lacking in utility. Caldwell and Spinks' list of benefits provides a clear, unambiguous statement about what policy can do for organizations and stakeholders. These benefits are further developed throughout this book.

Concluding Comment

This chapter has given an overview of what is meant by policy and what is meant by education policy studies. Also discussed were several definitions of policy along with the benefits of policy. These fundamental aspects of policy are important to understand as we explore various aspects of policy and policy-making in this text.

Chapter 2 examines the various values and principles inherent in education policy.

DISCUSSION/REFLECTION QUESTIONS

1. When you hear the word *policy*, what are your perceptions of its meaning?

2. Generally speaking, are people positive or negative when they hear the word *policy* being used? Explain your response.

3. How would you define education policy?

4. What is your concept of education policy studies?

5. Should educational practitioners and theorists be concerned about education policy studies? Why or why not?

6. Policy is sometimes referred to as the foundation of an organization. Is this true when we speak about educational organizations? Elaborate.

7. From your day-to-day work as an educator, what benefits of policy have you experienced? Have you also experienced drawbacks to policy? Explain them.

8. Keeping in mind Marshall and Gerstl-Pepin's (2005) comment that policies are the result of politics, explain how politics might have affected the development of a policy you may have personally experienced.

9. If you were designing a graduate course on education policy studies, what would you consider the key components of such a course? Justify their inclusion in your course outline.

2

Values and Principles
in Education Policy

The process of developing education policy, with all its concomitant processes, is an exercise fraught with a multitude of competing values and principles. Taylor, Rizvi, Lingard, and Henry (1997) spoke about the competing interests in the policy process and the reality that policies represent compromises over struggles (p. 26). This competitive nature, they further suggested, highlights the "value-laden nature of policies" (p. 27). Indeed, Prunty (1985) defined policy as "the authoritative allocation of values" (p. 136). With such a heavy emphasis on the importance of values, our discussion now turns to the role values play in the policy-making process.

Values

It is obvious that power and control are two primary values in the policy-making process. As to whose interests these values represent, Taylor et al. (1997) proffer the following cogent perspective:

> First there are those accounts which accept a dispersal of values and power throughout society and argue that governments attempt to please as many interest groups in the policy process as possible. This is the *pluralist approach*. In contrast, the *elitist approach* sees governments as acting in relation to the values and interests of dominant groups. *Neo-marxist approaches* take this position even further in arguing that those who "control" the economy have more political influence than others. Within such accounts there is a distinction between those who see this relationship as tightly deterministic and those who see it as more indirect—acknowledging that governments sometimes act against the interests of the economically powerful.

Feminist approaches may be pluralist, elitist, or neo-marxist but all see the state as operating to reproduce male interests and power. (p. 27)

Pal (1987) has suggested there are three types of values worth considering when dealing with public policy: content values, process values, and target group values. An examination of these values indicates their significant relevance to the study of education policy. Consider the following:

1. *Content values:* Pal perceived these values addressing what should be done. In educational decision-making, which is at the core of education policy-making, there exists the age-old debate of centralization versus decentralization. Should decisions be made by a core group or should the decision-making process be open to a much wider involvement on the part of stakeholders? School-based management represents a movement designed to involve grass-roots participation in decision-making.

2. *Process values:* Pal considered these values speaking to how to do something or, more specifically, how policies should be implemented and delivered. These are key questions that educators grapple with daily and consume a considerable amount of time, a commodity that is always in great demand in education.

3. *Target group values:* Pal described these values as "whom to do it for" (p. 209). As we have observed, by its very nature, the policy process is full of competing interests. The various groups involved in those competing interests will each claim that it is their specific group that is the most deserving. Pal speaks of two groups: those that are positively valued (such as women, the elderly, the very young, the handicapped, small farmers, small business, and racial and religious minorities) and those that are negatively valued (such as large business, large unions, and professionals). These groups have traditionally been neglected in the policy-making process and consequently may not be referred to in actual policies (p. 213).

These values are significant for educators and deserve closer scrutiny when we study policy-making, which is a complex, highly political process. One question always looms over the issue of values: in whose interests is policy made? I will discuss other values to consider in the paragraphs that follow.

Marshall, Mitchell, and Wirt (1989) posit four values they consider to be "subsumed in school policy":

1. *Quality:* This value is seen as "instrumental, a means to another value goal, namely the fulfillment of diverse human purposes, thereby making life worth living and individuals worthwhile."
2. *Efficiency:* This value "takes two forms, economic (minimizing costs while maximizing gains) and accountability (oversight and control of the local exercise of power)."
3. *Equity:* This value refers to "the use of political authority to redistribute critical resources required for the satisfaction of human needs."
4. *Choice:* This value refers to local school authorities having the opportunity either to make policy decisions or to reject them. (p. 82)

Although these are not the only values that should concern us as we develop policy, they are key when we are discussing schools and education. According to Sergiovanni, Burlingame, Coombs, and Thurston (1992),

> these are not the only values that enter into educational policy-making, but they are the four justifications for policies most frequently heard. Most of us prize each of these to some degree and, in fact, most policy issues involve more than one of them. Nevertheless, the position you take on issues will probably agree with your own sense of which values are most important. Which value you will defend most vigorously will depend on the role you play in the educational policy process as well as your own personal value hierarchy. (p. 223)

So we cannot pretend that policy-making is objective. Having recognized its political dimensions, we must also acknowledge its ethical and moral implications.

Pal (1992) emphasized the ethical dimension of policy and suggested that in policy debates, these ethical dimensions are either implied or presented directly. He went on to say that

> there are some policy areas where the ethical dimension appears muted, and others where it is the dominant chord. Economic policies, for example, are often discussed as though technical issues were paramount. Everyone appears to be in favor of economic growth; the question is how best, from a technical point of view, to stimulate that growth. Means cannot be divorced from ends, however, and each technical solution has consequences which may properly be judged on ethical grounds. Policy debates over discrimination, application of human rights legislation, education, culture, genetic engineering, abortion, and the family seem to hinge directly upon, or move very quickly to, issues of value such as freedom, individual rights,

the proper role of the state, and the obligations and responsibilities of society to protect human life. In short, matters related to human sexuality, the sanctity of life, and traditional freedoms of speech and expression are self-evidently moral and ethical ones, and are forthrightly discussed in those terms. (p. 207)

The role of ethics, not to mention the obvious presence of ethics in the actual policies being developed, is extremely important in the policy-making process. Educators and other students of policy must acknowledge and be highly cognizant of the fact that certain values will compete for attention in both the policy process and the policy product.

Fowler (2009) also suggested there may be several competing values inherent in the policy-making process. She categorized those values under the headings of self-interest values, general social values, democratic values, and economic values. Self-interest values include economic interests and power, while general social values include order and individualism. Fowler perceived liberty, equality, and fraternity coming under democratic values. Economic values encompass efficiency, economic growth, and quality (pp. 107–117). At first blush, these values may appear to be mutually exclusive because, as Fowler has stated, they may compete with each other; however, the perceived competition is ultimately healthy in that policy-makers are exposed to a variety of perspectives, which should—at least in theory—result in better, well-thought-out policies.

We now turn to a discussion of principles that are imbedded in those values.

Principles

In addition to the significance values hold in education policy studies, the subject of principles in education policy is also a topic of major consideration. The distinction between values and principles is sometimes blurred in various educational issues but nonetheless, it is imperative educators understand the differences when examining education policy. Values, as defined by Webster, refer to something regarded as desirable, worthy, or right as a belief, standard, or precept (Values, 1992, p. 1070). Principles, on the other hand, are defined as general truths or laws, basic to other truths (Principles, 1992, p. 770).

In education policy studies, values are exactly as the name suggests: standards or precepts the policy-maker considers so important that they permeate the specific policy. As we discussed earlier, the value of *choice* is an excellent example. Principles, on the other hand, are general truths that are kept in mind as policies are developed.

Gallagher (1992) saw principles as "decision criteria" that school boards and school administrators attempted to consider when developing and adopting new policies (p. 45). She suggested four such criteria or principles to keep in mind when discussing policy:

1. technical feasibility
2. economic and financial possibility
3. political viability
4. administrative operability

Let us review each of these principles briefly.

Technical feasibility criteria measure whether policy or program outcomes achieve their purpose (Gallagher, 1992, p. 46). In other words, does a particular policy work in the real world and accomplish what it is supposed to do? If it does, then it stands up to the test: it achieves or lives up to the principle of technical feasibility. Gallagher cautioned, however, that "when dealing with human behavior, no policy or program will always bring about its intended effect" (p. 46). This is an important point about human agency that we will return to below.

Economic and financial possibility measure two outcomes: the cost of policies and programs and the benefits of such policies and programs (Gallagher, 1992, p. 48). The key question here is whether the cost of developing and implementing the policy in question is justified in terms of the anticipated benefits and results: a literal cost–benefit analysis. One of the major criticisms of educational reform is that many reform initiatives are monetarily motivated and not driven by sound educational reasons. Policy is no exception to such thinking. There may be times in education when we have to "bite the bullet" and introduce policies that are questionable from an economic perspective but that are valid and extremely desirable from an educational standpoint. After all, we are dealing with the lives and futures of our most precious resource: our children. (The idea of operating in multiple time scales is another important point we will return to later.)

Political viability refers to whether a policy will "fly" given the various stakeholders involved. Education is highly politicized today, and if a policy is not acceptable to the relevant power groups, its successful implementation is in jeopardy. Support for the policy must come from these groups or the policy is in all probability doomed to failure. But who the power groups in a community may be is dynamic through time and location, so no single solution or understanding of this principle will work for all policy-makers or analysts.

Administrative operability refers to the practicality of a policy. Are the financial and human resources available to implement the policy? Will teachers support the policy? Is the staffing available? Are the physical facilities available? These are but a few of the questions that need to be looked at under this umbrella of administrative operability, and from these types of questions, we can see how the principle might be stressed.

Concluding Comment

When discussing values and principles on any subject in education, practitioners may become impatient. It is sometimes a challenge to see where values and principles fit in the larger picture of policy-making. This chapter has attempted to make that fit clear. It is imperative practitioners see "the big picture" because values and principles are intricately intertwined in all aspects of education policy, including those that affect the daily work of teachers and administrators.

Although it is relatively easy to approach and discuss policy from a linear perspective, any discussion of policy in real life is indeed tangly and even convoluted—anything but linear and straightforward. This chapter, and this book as a whole, is an attempt to break down that "tangliness," that "convolutedness," by presenting policy and its myriad aspects in as pragmatic a fashion as possible. Chapter 3 examines the various types of education policies.

DISCUSSION/REFLECTION QUESTIONS

1. Taylor et al. (1997) spoke about the "value-laden nature of policies" (p. 27). Is this an appropriate descriptor of education policies? Elaborate.

2. Do you think power and control are inherent in the policy-making process? Explain.

3. Quality, efficiency, equity, and choice permeate the literature on education policy as key values. Choose a policy you have had some involvement in as an educator and discuss that policy in terms of these four values.

4. Technical feasibility, economic and financial possibility, political viability, and administrative operability are, according to Gallagher (1992), four important decision criteria to consider when we discuss policy in general. Do these criteria apply to education policy?

Consider an education policy you are aware of that was unsuccessful in implementation; discuss that lack of success in terms of these four decision criteria.

5. School boards and ministries of education are key agencies involved in education policy-making. From your experience, do you perceive these agencies to be cognizant of the "value-laden nature of policies" (Taylor et al., 1997, p. 27), and if they are, how do you think this awareness affects their role as policy developers? If they are not cognizant of the "value-laden nature of policies," how does that lack of awareness affect their role as policy developers?

6. How do you perceive the role of ethics in current policy development by school boards and ministries of education?

3

Types of Education Policies

There is indeed a preponderance of categorizations of policies in the academic literature, each contingent on the perspectives of the writers and researchers in this field. Although there is no definitive categorization or typology, each categorization has specific merits as it provides the student of policy with a variety of insights valuable to a holistic comprehension of policy from a macro point of view. The gleanings from these various insights and perspectives are instrumental in helping us to arrive at our own conceptions of what policy is all about.

Clemmer (1991) stated "there are many kinds of policies and they can be classified in many different ways, including purpose, subject, breadth of application, and derivation" (p. 164). He then goes on to categorize policies into four types: consequential, de facto, delegated, and formal (p. 164). A brief explanation of each type follows.

Consequential Policies

Consequential policies are those "activated by several factors" (Clemmer, 1991, p. 164). Such policies often result from outside forces or pressures such as provincial/state legislative actions. For example, if a government budget demands severe financial cutbacks, a ministry of education may be reluctant to introduce a policy that would require spending a great deal of money. Another example might be an ultraconservative school board refusing to introduce liberal policies regarding LGBT (lesbian, gay, bisexual, transgender) students in schools because professional staff members are wary of offending school trustees. Clemmer saw these forces or pressures as imposing "controls and requirements that significantly affect the policies of local school districts" (p. 164).

De Facto Policies

De facto policies are "assumed from actions employees see about them which the viewers believe to constitute policy" (Clemmer, 1991, p. 164). These policies develop where no official or stated policy is written down and might be referred to as "unofficial policy" for lack of a better name. Over time, these unofficial policies seem to become legitimated. As a consequence, de facto policies may be particularly resistant to change. We might look to students wearing ball caps as an example of a de facto policy. Students may have been prohibited from wearing ball caps in school years ago, when student dress was an issue; in today's society, however, dress in general seems to be less of a priority while other issues, such as drug use and the expression of sexual identity, to mention just a couple, are much greater priorities. Over time, earlier policies and practices tend to become institutionalized for a variety of reasons, one being the conservatism of faculties and staffs, which promotes and perpetuates "the good old days" way of thinking.

Delegated Policies

Delegated policies stem "from what is known in organizational circles as upward delegation" (Clemmer, 1991, p. 165). They emerge in situations where administrators do not know how a particular matter should be handled and so the responsibility for a decision is "sent upstairs" to a superior. Delegated policies are fairly common as it is practically impossible to have a formal or official policy on everything that occurs in a school district on a daily basis.

Formal Policies

Formal policies are those that are consciously and officially developed by an organization, such as a school district or an individual school. Clemmer (1991) described this type of policy as going "through the formulation process of all formal policies, opportunity for public involvement, submission of administrative recommendations, and thorough review by all board members before adoption" (p. 166). This is the ideal way to develop policy; some might even refer to this as the "textbook method" of policy development. Note its linearity, its very straightforwardness. An example of a formal policy might be a school board deciding to develop a homework policy for junior and senior high school students. Research is done by professional staff, findings are presented to trustees, trustees sanction the idea of developing a district-wide policy, and then the process of consultation with various stakeholders (i.e., administrators, teachers, parents and, we hope, junior and senior high school students) begins, culminating in a workable policy that has the approval of the majority of stakeholders.

An Australian Classification

Another way of classifying policies is that of "utilising binary distinctions" put forth by Australian policy researchers Taylor et al. (1997, p. 33). They explained that "it is sometimes possible to classify an actual policy as manifesting characteristics of the two arms of the binary distinction within a category" (p. 33). This type of policy is not all that common, but it does exist. Consider, for example, the homework policy referred to in the previous section. A possible binary distinction might be conservative–liberal, which is manifested through the policy having conservative aspects (such as an underlying premise that homework is beneficial to students) while at the same time having liberal aspects (such as dictating that the maximum amount of homework requires no more than one hour of a student's out-of-school time). The distinctions identified by Taylor et al. (1997) are distributive and redistributive, symbolic and material, rational and incremental, substantive and procedural, and regulatory and deregulatory.

Distributive vs. redistributive

Taylor et al. (1997) made the following distinctions between distributive and redistributive policies:

> Distributive policies involve straightforward allocation of resources or benefits or entitlements, for example if an allowance is provided for all students for school books or uniforms. However, if such an allowance is provided to a target group through means testing, the policy could be said to be redistributive in character. Many special needs policies are of this redistributive nature, for example additional resources granted to schools under the Disadvantaged Schools Programme in Australia. Other redistributive policies would include special allowances made available for geographically isolated students to attend boarding schools. (p. 33)

In a similar vein, Marshall and Gerstl-Pepin (2005) discussed the differences between redistributive policies and developmental policies:

> Sometimes policy makers attempt to make huge and fundamental structural alterations in education systems, and sometimes they

decide to work toward gradual change. Developmental programs are those in which most governments are involved anyway (e.g., transportation, education), so government initiatives tinker with the current system, making small changes, tending to reinforce local initiatives and provide extra resources, especially when there are new requirements. These get implemented fairly quickly with relatively little contention. Redistributive programs (e.g., special education, compensatory education) require that those working at the local school level engage in activities that require special services to certain designated clients but not others. Even as such policies are formulated, they provoke controversy; they are often resented, viewed as taking away from some to give to others. (p. 43)

Again let us use the example of a homework policy. Teachers might resent such a policy because they perceive a loss of autonomy if the amount of homework they can assign to students is limited to a one-hour time frame. Parents, on the other hand, may feel they have gained greater autonomy.

Symbolic vs. material

The distinction between symbolic and material refers to the extent of commitment to implementation by those responsible for formulating a given policy. Symbolic policies are those developed for "cosmetic" reasons; they are put into place to make an organization look good to the public. Material policies include a commitment to implementation through the provision of resources, whereas such a commitment is absent from symbolic policies. Symbolic policies tend to have broad, vague, ambiguous, abstract goal statements with little or no resource commitment and little thought given to implementation strategies. Indeed, the extent of resource commitment will often tell us much about the extent of political support for a given policy. A good example of a symbolic policy is Newfoundland and Labrador's 2013 *Safe and Caring Schools* policy. This policy was developed in response to bullying and aggressive student behavior and is most eloquent in its platitudes espousing safe and caring schools. In reality, however, there have been numerous examples throughout the province of student brutality toward teachers, yet school administrators and school board officials are reluctant to take corrective action to deal with the issue.

In general, then, symbolic policies are weaker than material policies. However, it should not be thought that symbolic policies are necessarily unimportant. Symbolic policies can perform a strategic function in legitimizing the views of certain groups and altering the political climate in which issues are discussed. The development of a symbolic policy may be the first stage of an ongoing political strategy. Once an issue gets onto the policy agenda, pressure can subsequently be directed at strengthening the policy and the financial commitment to it—depending upon the extent of political support for the policy in the electorate. (Taylor et al., 1997, p. 34)

Rational vs. incremental

Taylor et al. (1997) had this to say about rational and incremental approaches to policy:

> rational advocates outline a set of prescriptive stages for the development of policy. On the other hand, incrementalists argue that policy development works over time by building on currently existing policies and practices. Even with a change of government, incrementalists argue that policy usually defines itself in relation to what went before. (p. 34)

Both rational and incremental approaches have their place in policy-making and are common in organizations. I prefer the rational approach because it is more transparent and allows policy-makers to start from "ground zero," whereas the incremental approach may carry with it negative baggage not easily jettisoned.

Substantive vs. procedural

Another distinction proffered by Taylor et al. (1997) is that of substantive and procedural:

> Substantive policies deal with what governments are intending to do, and procedural policies with how things are to be done and by whom. For example, the Queensland Department of Education's Social Justice Strategy was developed in the early 1990s in the form of a brief rationale and statement of principles. As such, it could be said at that stage to have been a substantive policy. When it was fully developed with resources and guidelines for implementation, it could also be classified as a procedural policy because it outlined responsibilities for implementation across the system. (pp. 34–35)

For a good policy, it seems to me that both substantive and procedural aspects are highly desirable. By *substantive* I mean that the policy has real essence, and by *procedural* I mean that the policy includes realistic steps to help in its implementation.

Regulatory vs. deregulatory

Regulatory and deregulatory are the final distinctions suggested by Taylor et al. (1997):

> Policies in the equity and social justice area tend to be of a *regulatory* character, that is, they are about controlling practices. Thus, for example, sexual harassment policy seeks to prohibit certain behaviors. By contrast, *deregulatory* policies are usually associated with an ideological commitment to minimal government—or state intervention often associated with the release of market forces. Such policies are not concerned with overt control, though more subtle mechanisms of control may emerge in devolved systems. (p. 35)

Ideally, policies are designed to provide guidance and direction—in other words, to provide a degree of flexibility in decision-making. In devolved systems, however, where decision-making is more commonly done at the site level (e.g., in the school building), some friction may exist between regulatory and deregulatory policies, depending, of course, on the philosophies of policy-making espoused by local school administrators. We often perceive regulatory and deregulatory policies to be in conflict with each other, but it is important to realize that both perspectives are common in the world of policy-making and each has its role to play. That role is unique to the specific context of a particular policy.

Effect Category

Policies are often categorized according to their effect. Clemmer's (1991) categories classified policies in terms of what they want to accomplish. Specifically, those categories are restrictive, nonrestrictive, prescriptive, and definitive policies. Here is a brief description of each category.

Restrictive

Restrictive policies are meant to narrow the operational choices of those who will implement them while allowing freedom to act within prescribed limits. Clemmer (1991) presented some cautions when these kinds of policies are being considered:

> Such restrictions can be based on past experience or defensible apprehension but they should not reflect the special bias of one particularly conservative or liberal board member, nor should they imply that the board distrusts its administrators (even if it is true). When capable superintendents begin to feel unnecessarily hamstrung by policy restrictions, they become understandably restive. Restrictions

on staff choices are not unreasonable (to allow total freedom is to
invite anarchy), but whenever possible they should be reserved for
administrative regulations and imposed sparingly at the policy level.
(p. 171)

Nonrestrictive

The opposite of restrictive policies, nonrestrictive policies are intended
"to capitalize on the most professional and creative impulses of district
employees at all levels" (Clemmer, 1991, p. 171). These are perceived in a
positive light:

> They perform an enabling function and allow for the broadest
> ranges of personal judgment. It is like telling the children they have
> full choice in what they watch but you expect them to show good
> judgment, adding that you do not expect the older ones to simply
> take over and impose inappropriate programs on their less powerful
> siblings, and that each is at liberty to choose something else to do.
> In short, nonrestrictive policies express a board's implicit trust in the
> judgment of its administration. (p. 171)

Prescriptive

Prescriptive policies are used "where the board wishes to direct staff's
actions, allowing virtually no deviations among schools or personnel"
(Clemmer, 1991, p. 171). Again, Clemmer cautioned against the use of
such policies:

> School district employees who view themselves as professionals—
> that's most of them in most districts—will tolerate the imposition of
> only a few prescriptive policies before becoming resentful. (In fact,
> the advent of collective bargaining in public education can prob-
> ably be attributed more to unwarranted impositions on professional
> prerogatives than any other single factor.) Prescriptive policies reveal
> a patronizing attitude that—until adolescence—is more acceptable
> in a parent–child relationship than in one involving only adults who
> want to be viewed as co-contributors to a worthy enterprise. (p. 172)

Definitive

According to Clemmer (1991), definitive policies define or describe terms
or conditions which, if not explained, might lead to confusion or incon-
sistency in implementation. A good example of this category is the following: "For purposes of field trips and transportation elementary school
pupils shall mean those in grades kindergarten through eight" (p. 172).

This is a policy because it emanates from the board and it is descriptive because it defines a term that appears in other policies (p. 172).

McDonnell and Elmore Classification

One final method of categorizing types of policies is worthy of mention. Based on their research into the policy-making process, McDonnell and Elmore (cited in Odden, 1991) have developed four such types: mandates, inducements, capacity-building, and system-changing.

Mandates

Mandates refer to policies intended to produce compliance. According to McDonnell and Elmore,

> the benefits of mandates sometimes accrue primarily to specific individuals or groups, as for example, when handicapped or disadvantaged students benefit from federal or state-mandated programs in local schools. Often mandates are intended to benefit a broader community or society as a whole, as, for example, when polluters are required to install abatement equipment to reduce bad air or water. (cited in Odden, 1991, pp. 164–165)

An example of such a policy might involve a conservative school district having a policy whereby transgender students are required to use the school washroom of their birth sex. It would be an understatement to say that this policy is meant to produce compliance!

Inducements

McDonnell and Elmore defined inducements as "transfers of money to individuals or agencies in return for the production of goods or services" (cited in Odden, 1991, p. 165). They stated that

> because inducements are conditional grants for money, they are frequently accompanied by rules (often called regulations) designed to assure that money is used consistently with policy-makers' intent . . . . The benefits of inducements accrue both to implementing agencies in the form of increased budget and authority, and to individual beneficiaries, through the value that is produced by the implementing agency. (p. 165)

Organizations such as ministries of education often develop policies with financial incentives (i.e., inducements) to schools in order to encourage schools to enact some initiative that is perceived to be of benefit to its stakeholders. For instance, it is not uncommon for the government of the day, prior to an election, to disperse considerable sums of money to curry favor with the local electorate. Another pertinent example might involve the concept of computer literacy. Schools are given a fixed sum with which to purchase updated computer software and hardware for students to use during school and after the school day ends. Parents may also be given the opportunity to use this equipment after regular school hours.

Capacity-building

A third policy type is capacity-building. Used when mandates and inducements are ineffective, investments in material, intellectual, or human resources become a policy option and are referred to as capacity-building (Clemmer, 1991). Let me give an example of this type of policy. A ministry of education, preoccupied with a larger governmental focus on health and wellness in order to reduce provincial/state health expenditures, develops a policy to provide schools with an abundance of physical exercise equipment. A number of schools may actually lack the physical space to accommodate this equipment, resulting in much of it being left in the original shipping cartons, unused. Capacity-building in theory, but a significant waste of money in reality! McDonnell and Elmore saw the benefits of capacity-building accruing "in the short term to the specific individuals and the institutions that are their recipients, but the ultimate beneficiaries are future members of society, whose interests cannot be clearly determined in the present" (cited in Odden, 1991, p. 166).

System-changing

The final policy type articulated by McDonnell and Elmore is system-changing:

> the transfer of official authority among individuals and agencies. The expected effect of system-broadening or narrowing is a change in the institutional structure by which public goods and services are delivered and often a change in the incentives which determine the nature and effects of those goods and services. (cited in Odden, 1991, p. 166)

Here is an example. A private school has decided that it lacks the financial and human resources to work with students who are cognitively delayed and severely cognitively impaired. Consequently, none of these students are now permitted to attend that school. Most educators believe that inclusion has many positive aspects, not only for the students included but also for the students in what might be referred to as the regular stream. So the overall effect of the private school's policy for students, both those permitted to attend the school and those excluded from attending, is negative. Opportunities to develop positive attributes such as healthy self-esteem, empathy, and a sense of caring and concern for others are jeopardized and perhaps lost to both groups of students.

Concluding Comment

This chapter has discussed a variety of ways to categorize policies. Many similarities and differences characterize these categorizations. No matter what the category, it is incumbent upon the policy-maker and students of policy-making to think carefully through what a policy endeavors to accomplish. Education policy analysis is the focus of chapter 4.

DISCUSSION/REFLECTION QUESTIONS

1. Clemmer (1991), McDonnell and Elmore (1991), and Taylor et al. (1997) have offered various categorizations for classifying policies. Compare and contrast any two of these classification systems.

2. Of these various categorizations for classifying policies, does one appeal to you more than the others? If so, which one and why?

3. What, if any, are the practical benefits of classifying policies? Elaborate.

4. In addition to the classifications discussed in this chapter, can you suggest any other policy classification systems?

4

Policy Analysis

There is no shortage of definitions for policy analysis. This section examines several of those definitions and then considers various forms of analysis. A couple of practical models of analysis are also presented for consideration.

Policy Analysis Defined

Gallagher (1992) proffered this explanation of what education policy analysis is all about:

> In its most general sense, *policy analysis* is the process of locating information relevant to the identified purpose. In this broad sense, *policy analysis* is synonymous with *problem solving.* Policy analysis has two characteristic features: the information collected has a practical orientation and the information will help guide action rather than be an end in itself. So the aim of policy analysis is to provide decision makers with information that can be used to make reasoned judgments in finding solutions to practical problems. (p. 4)

Gallagher's perception of policy analysis is a basic, straightforward one, easily understandable to the less academic among us. There are, however, other definitions of policy analysis out there that are more erudite and run deeper.

In his work on education policy, Downey (1988) referred to policy analysis as "the generation of information for the purpose of informing the policy-making process" (p. 12). He then suggested that this information gathering usually consists of the following activities:

1. time-series, time-specific studies of trends and situation-specific studies, either of the school system itself or of its

environment, for purposes of alerting school boards to the need
for policy change;

2. the crafting of policy alternatives in response to the
   demonstrated need for policy change; and

3. estimations of feasibility to help governing boards assess
   the consequences of adopting various policy alternatives.
   (pp. 12–13)

Taking a more holistic approach, Sandell (1977) referred to policy
analysis as "a set of procedures for inventing, anticipating, exploring,
comparing, and articulating the alternatives available for achieving certain objectives. It is a method of managing . . . collecting and organizing
. . . information. It is an effort to ease the consternation that stems from
seeking better ways to ordain the process of decision making" (p. 48). This
definition may be somewhat informative to practitioners in the field, but
otherwise is not very helpful. It is included here to point out the range
of perspectives on policy analysis and to underscore that some of those
perspectives may lack utility.

Pal (1987) took a more erudite approach to defining policy analysis
when he stated that it is "the disciplined application of intellect to public
problems" (p. 19). He explained two key features of policy analysis. First,
policy analysis is a cognitive activity; it is about learning and thinking.
Second, policy analysis, as part of the collective policy process, is itself
a collective activity. Thus, if policy problems are not thought through
dynamically, we have not engaged in analysis.

More recently, Pal (1997) quoted an explanation of policy analysis
from one of his interviewees:

> [Policy analysis is] a way of thinking, an ability to sift the extraneous
> from the essential, to get to the bottom, to see patterns and connec-
> tions such as historical or international comparisons. It's the ability
> to think ahead a few moves, about the consequences downstream.
> It's the ability to organize information. (p. 15)

Taking a similarly pragmatic view of policy analysis, Williams (1982)
conceptualized the term as "a means of synthesizing information including research results to produce a format for policy decisions (the laying
out of alternative choices) and of determining future needs for policy-
relevant information" (p. ix). In that same vein, Quade (1975) wrote that
"policy analysis searches for feasible courses of action, generating information and marshaling evidence of the benefits and other consequences
that would follow their adoption and implementation, in order to help

the policymaker choose the most advantageous action" (p. 5). Note, then, that policy analysis may be just as practical as it is rational: not critique for the sake of critique but rather a search for what works best in a given situation.

According to Colebatch (1998), policy analysis "commonly consists of techniques for identifying alternative courses of action, estimating their likely outcomes, and calculating which alternative best accomplishes known goals . . . . These calculations yield 'objective' conclusions in support of one particular course of action" (p. 83). He further explained that

> this assumes that organizations exist to pursue goals, these goals
> are clear, and that the best way to pursue them is a technical matter
> which can be left to the experts. All of these assumptions are debat-
> able. While it is assumed that organizations have goals, it is not
> always clear in practice what they are, how they have been chosen, or
> that organizational activity is best explained as an attempt to achieve
> these goals. And even if there are clear goals, it is not clear that par-
> ticipants are prepared to accept the judgement of an independent
> policy analyst about the best way to achieve them: policy inquiry
> appears to be about interaction and negotiation rather than about
> scientific detachment. (p. 83)

Colebatch's explanation of policy analysis is reasonable and lines up to some extent with the next approach to policy, suggested by Ball.

In his discussions on policy analysis, Ball (1994) suggested an open and creative approach that involves finding the appropriate theory and concepts for the specific task in question. He observed: "The task, then, is to examine the moral order of reform and the relationship of reform to existing patterns of social inequality, bringing to bear those concepts and interpretive devices which offer the best possibilities of insight and understanding" (p. 2). Notice that this approach acknowledges the political and ethical dimensions we touched on earlier.

Taylor et al. (1997) offered an acute insight into what policy analysis is all about:

> In doing policy analysis, we need to keep in mind a distinction
> between policy *per se* and the substantive issues with which a specific
> policy deals . . . . Some analysts suggest that the very first task in pol-
> icy analysis is to focus on the issue itself. There is a need to do this
> so we are able to assess how the policy is likely to work in relation to
> the problems it is addressing . . . . However, given that policy is often
> as much about problem setting as problem solving, there are often
> difficulties in separating the policy and the issues, because policies
> frame policy issues in particular ways. (pp. 39–40)

Policy analysis must be done in a systematic, organized way. Moving along the policy-development continuum, however, can be a complex process—and a challenging one at that.

Alexander (2013) suggested this pragmatic and succinct definition:

> Policy analysis is a method of inquiry, a process by which we try to make the world a better place. It is a journey that begins with identifying something wrong with our surroundings, and it ends with a resolution or alleviation of that problematic condition. (p. 5)

However, in his seminal work on policy analysis, Wildavsky (1979) confronted attempts to define policy analysis absolutely:

> there can be no one definition of policy analysis. As old-time cooks used to say when asked how much spice a recipe required, "as much as it takes." Policy analysis is an applied sub-field whose content cannot be determined by disciplinary boundaries but by whatever appears appropriate to the circumstances of the time and the nature of [the] problem . . . . Do not ask from me what you should not want—a definitive definition of policy analysis good for all times, places, and circumstances. (p. 15)

Whether you believe policy analysis is a method or an activity, something quantifiable or something ineffable, it is resolutely *something*. We can classify it further by examining forms of policy analysis.

Forms of Policy Analysis

As we established in the previous section, there is no one way of defining policy analysis. The same can be said when we examine the various forms of policy analysis. But first let us consider the basis of policy analysis.

Downey (1988) explained the information-generating activities associated with policy analysis like this:

> (1) the development of the accumulating data characteristic of traditional planning and management information systems; (2) the conduct of here-and-now evaluations of institutions or assessments of community needs; and (3) studies of the likely costs and benefits of specific policy changes. (p. 13)

He continued:

> Analysis, then, in its broadest sense, can be *descriptive* of ongoing trends, *appraisive* of existing conditions, and *anticipatory* of the consequences of possible policy changes. When analysis generates such information, it serves as the intelligence system for the policy making process. (p. 13)

These key descriptors reflect forms of policy analysis. Pal (1987) spoke about the three similar, general styles of policy analysis: descriptive, process, and evaluation. He stated that these three styles "simply reflect orientations or intellectual postures toward policy questions" (p. 28). His description of each style follows. (See Pal, 1987, pp. 27–37, for further details.)

Descriptive analysis

This form of analysis encompasses both content analysis and historical analysis.

Content analysis is, in one sense, the most pedestrian type of analysis, but it is also one of the most important and is frequently neglected. It provides an empirical description of the content of an existing public policy, in terms of its intentions, problem definition, goals, and instruments.

Any description of current policy requires at least a modest review of immediately preceding events. Historical analysis, however, goes well beyond simply examining immediate antecedents. Instead, it assumes that current public policies can be fully understood only by examining their evolution, preferably from their inception in modern times.

Process analysis

Process analysis focuses on the immediate political process, decisions, debates, conflicts, and compromises that produce public policy. It pays less detail to content and its evolution and more to the process whereby that content is determined. Policy is seen as an outcome, and while process analysis certainly tries to provide a clear sketch of policy content, its main interest is in how the content came to be.

Evaluation analysis

Rather than describing or explaining, evaluation analysis aims in varying degrees at judging. It may judge logical consistency, efficiency, or ethical character.

Logical evaluation is similar to content analysis in that it examines the current, detailed content of public policy. Rather than simply describing, however, logical analysis assesses a policy's internal rigor and consistency.

Public policies are problem-solving tools, so a major task of policy analysis is to gauge whether they work. *Empirical evaluation* adopts a wide range of techniques to assess the efficiency and efficacy of a public policy. Whereas as logical policy evaluation also considers the likely consequences of policies, empirical evaluation includes a type of impact analysis. The distinguishing feature of empirical evaluation, however, is a concerted attempt to discover what the "real" effects are. Empirical inquiry replaces conjecture.

Ethical evaluation assesses policies in terms of pre-existing value systems of right and wrong. Many economic policies seem immune to this sort of analysis, hinging instead on questions of technical efficiency in reaching agreed-on goals such as lower inflation or increased investment. Other policy issues seem more obviously situated on an ethical terrain: prostitution, pornography, gay rights, school prayer, foreign aid to corrupt or cruel regimes, and abortion, for example. The difference between these ethically charged and technical policies, however, is more apparent than real. Efficiency, that shibboleth of apparently technical public policies, is entirely without ethical content, and so cannot be valued for its own sake. Concentration camps, for instance, can be models of efficiency, but are devoid of justice. On a more pedestrian level, an economic policy that encourages maximum labor productivity might countenance working conditions that undermine human dignity.

Here is one final comment by Pal (1987) on the various styles of policy analysis:

> Good analysis is always grounded in solid description and historical understanding, though it may focus on logic, efficiency, efficacy, or ethics. As well, good policy analysis is usually comparative. Comparison does not constitute a style of its own, but is the deliberate selection of instances and counter-instances from other times and places. Comparison shows what is unique or routine about a given policy or policy proposal, and provides a broader canvas for assessment. (p. 37)

Policy analysis is an intricate part of policy development. I have presented the various forms of policy analysis in linear form for the purposes of illustration and clarity. It is important to realize, however, that in the field, practitioners are likely to encounter a hybrid of these forms. Which aspects will be used depends on the context of the policy in question.

In the next section, we consider some specific models that operationalize the aspects of analysis we have just discussed.

Policy Analysis Models

Gallagher (1992) suggested a model for conducting policy analysis—CASA, which stands for Clear And Simple Analysis and is made up of five steps:

Step 1: Identifying the problem
Step 2: Defining policy decision criteria
Step 3: Developing policy alternatives
Step 4: Considering policy alternatives
Step 5: Presenting the policy choices (pp. 6–12)

Let us review these steps in detail.

Identifying the problem

At first blush, this step would appear to be relatively simple. However, the complexities of the situation might prove otherwise. Gallagher (1992) clarified:

> Because conditions change, the policy analyst must continually ask whether the problem that precipitated the search for a solution still exists. Often the analyst has to redefine the problem during analysis as it changes form or takes on new dimensions. In following the CASA model, the school policy analyst will analyze the best data available about the problem, settle on the criteria that will be used to evaluate alternative policies, think up possible alternatives, and then redefine the problem so that it can be reduced, controlled, and perhaps resolved with the information and resources on hand. Such an approach is often demanded by the immediacy of the problems found in public education and the short period during which the analysis must be conducted. (pp. 6–7)

Policies are ideally developed from a proactive stance, but in reality, many policies are developed from a reactive position. The commonality in both perspectives is that there is a problem, whether it has already happened or is perceived as about to happen. Once the existence of the problem has been determined, a policy is needed for resolution. What remains then is to define our criteria.

Defining policy decision criteria

A multitude of criteria exist for decision-makers to consider when developing new policies or revising old ones. These criteria may include financial considerations, legalities, political acceptability, efficiency, administrative ease or convenience, and efficiency (Gallagher, 1992). Part of policy analysis may involve recognizing and explaining the factors that shaped a policy.

Gallagher (1992) offered this sage advice to the policy analyst:

> Seldom are decision criteria of equal value to policymakers. The analyst will have to identify those criteria that are central to the

problem under analysis and most relevant to the key participants in the decision process. Clarification of decision criteria early in the process helps to avoid the temptation to rationalize preferred options later. Similar to the ongoing nature of problem identification, new decision criteria may be unearthed during later steps of the analysis. (p. 9)

Developing policy alternatives

Having gone through steps one and two, the policy analyst now has to develop several alternatives to present to the decision-makers. Gallagher (1992) cautioned that "the challenge at this step in the CASA model is *to avoid prematurely limiting the number of policy options*" (p. 10).

How does the policy analyst go about developing these alternatives? Gallagher (1992) made these suggestions:

The analyst has several methods available: library research to find out what others have done, talking to experts (both other school officials and national consultants), and brainstorming . . . . As values and assumptions of participants change over time, yesterday's unacceptable policy option may be today's consensus choice. (p. 10)

The policy analyst must keep an open mind: the analyst's thinking must be flexible, creative, and responsive to any issue that may arise.

Considering policy alternatives

After several policy alternatives have been developed, the analyst must consider those alternatives in light of the identified problem and decision criteria. Gallagher (1992) had this to say:

Careful consideration of alternatives will weed out realistic policy choices from pie-in-the-sky choices. Some alternatives may satisfy many decision criteria. Other alternatives can be discarded at this point because they violate the most salient decision criteria . . . . At this step in CASA, the analyst may discover the problem has changed or that it no longer exists. This often can occur when the problem identification step resulted in inaccurate or incomplete analysis. This is not necessarily a negative development, however. It simply confirms the suggestion that, because the first attempt at problem identification is done quickly, several iterations through CASA will result in more relevant choices. (p. 11)

Having arrived at a number of policy options, the analyst must next present those options to the organization or agency (i.e., the client) in need of the policy.

Presenting the policy choices

This fifth step in the CASA model is determined by "the relationship between the analyst and the policymaking body (the client)" (Gallagher, 1992, p. 11). That body may simply ask the analyst to present two or three viable options with the positives and negatives of each option. Or the client may request all the policy alternatives be presented with the pros and cons of each and then make a decision based on that information.

Gallagher (1992) expounded on this process:

> In cases where the board of education is faced with competing political groups, and little consensus about anything exists, the analyst may lay out the options by displaying the political pros and cons. Use of political feasibility analysis can answer questions like these: What will the board have to give up or promise to have the policy alternative implemented? Will new administrative structures be required? Does the board have the influence to implement a more comprehensive alternative as opposed to an alternative that solves part of the problem? Rarely is there one "best" alternative. Not only will different alternatives appeal to different political groups, but more than one alternative may solve the identified problem. Because making the policy choice is only part of the decision-making process, the policy analyst can help the decision makers consider the tasks and responsibilities involved in planning for the implementation and evaluation of the final choice. (p. 12)

Gallagher's approach to policy analysis is practical, workable, and incremental. We now examine a different model, put forth by Brown (1996).

The Realistic Model

Another policy analysis model worthy of consideration is the Realistic Model for Policy Analysis as developed by Brown (1996). Brown used the image of the web to explain the intricacies of this model: "At the center of the web is a tangled core, the problem area (1). Radiating out from it, there is an intricate pattern of policy analysis, which requires clarification (2), decision-making (3), and finally problem formation (4)" (p. 21). A brief discussion of each of these areas follows.

The problem area

With a preponderance of conflict involving values and goals in the policymaking process, Brown (1996) concluded that "it is little wonder that the problem area is messy, confused and poorly understood" (p. 22). She recommended that when first confronted with a problem area, policy analysts need to try to clarify what it is all about. Think of this task as mapping the area or surveying the terrain before you jump fully into the work.

Clarification

Brown (1996) perceived the clarification component as a "cognitive process that will require policy analysts to read, listen, interpret, learn, persuade, [and] reflect" (p. 23). Specifically, there will be a need to study existing policies and interests, review available literature on the subject, search for new information, and establish parameters (p. 23). This step necessarily bounds and refines the identification of the problem area.

Decision-making

Decision-making is best understood as a process, not a single event. Brown (1996) observes that education policy analysts make many decisions from a perspective of ignorance (p. 25). She said further,

> these decisions are interpreted, based on facts, values, and motivations, and are debated with other policy analysts/policy makers who hold conflicting interpretations. The clarification cycle referred to in the second component may be entered and re-entered many times, depending on the level and intensity of the debate. Tentative decisions will be made, but there will be a search to falsify, to look for and learn from errors. (p. 25)

While an iterative decision-making process may seem inefficient, it is actually necessary if the analyst and the organization want to avoid a bad decision—a genuine risk when human group dynamics are in play.

Problem formation

According to Brown (1996), the end of the process of policy analysis is a tentative formulation of the problem and the solutions. As she explained,

> in the final step, then, analysts provide the best interpretation that they can of the problem, and then put forward the solution. It is given cautiously, fully realizing that there will be an on-going search to falsify parts or all of it, that errors will be found, although it is as error-free as analysts can present it at this stage. It will ask for monitoring so that errors can be identified and modified as quickly as possible. (p. 26)

But as with most processes in human life, the end of the analysis represents the beginning of a new step, as we will discuss in the next chapter.

Tips for Good Policy Analysis

Pal (1992) has offered several valuable tips for good policy analysis with the caveat that such "tips will not necessarily guarantee good work but ignoring them is almost certain to lead to shoddy analysis" (p. 277). (See Pal, 1992, pp. 277–280, for further details.)

1. *Dive deep.* Good analysis is almost always distinguished by a solid historical grasp of the issues and the problem. In other words, avoid superficiality by going in depth into all aspects of a specific policy.

2. *Know the law.* Be familiar with the laws involved in the substance of the policy. For instance, if a policy on negligence and liability is being developed, ensure the policy is congruent with the law in these areas.

3. *Count the stakes.* Every public policy is set against a political context of winners and losers, values and interests. Be sure to consider all these aspects, but ultimately, decisions have to be made. Remember that not everyone will be perfectly satisfied with the final product.

4. *Look at the big picture.* Practical policy analysis is usually undertaken at a specific level (e.g., *Should these subsidies be revised? Should this program be changed?*). It is tempting to keep one's analytical nose down in the dirt and not look up at the bigger picture, the long-term trends. A thoughtful look at the wider context is essential if analysis is to be imaginative, bold, and fresh.

5. *Be cautiously skeptical of experts.* If you are an expert in a specific field, it is difficult to be objective about what goes on in that field. Still, it is therefore important to try to keep a skeptical mind when you analyze policy.

6. *Be cautiously respectful of common sense.* Never underestimate how important common sense is, especially in the midst of the complicated and tangly phrasing often used in policy development.

7. *If possible, have a bias toward small solutions.* We often look for the big, complicated answers when we analyze policy, but very often the answers lie in basic and straightforward solutions.

8. *Choose policy targets you have a reasonable chance of controlling.* Some targets may not be obtainable. You have to be reasonable

and realistic in assessing which targets are obtainable and which ones are not.

9. *Try to structure choice into policy.* It is imperative to provide significant choice in policy-making; no choice is restrictive and takes away the proactive aspect of policy.

10. *Be balanced in considering interests, but err on the side of diffuse interests over concentrated, organized interests.* Public policy should serve the greater good, hence the importance of ethics in policy development.

Concluding Comment

In this chapter, multiple definitions of policy analysis have been presented as well as a couple of forms or styles of policy analysis. To bring this topic down to an operational level, two policy analysis models were proffered for consideration along with several tips on how to achieve good policy analysis. The next chapter looks at the actual development of policy.

DISCUSSION/REFLECTION QUESTIONS

1. Does policy analysis happen in the real world of education?

2. What factors might impede effective policy analysis? How might some of the impediments be overcome?

3. Compare and contrast Gallagher's (1992) and Brown's (1996) models of policy analysis.

4. Does thorough policy analysis ensure successful policy? Elaborate.

5. Pal's (1992) tips for good policy analysis speak to policy in general. How applicable are these tips to education policy? Discuss using specific examples from your everyday work as an educator.

6. What practical suggestions might you offer to improve the policy analysis process?

5

Policy Development

The actual crafting of policy is referred to as policy development. Policy development is "not a one-time activity" (Clemmer, 1991, p. 54) and is undertaken as a long-term process. Taylor et al. (1997) suggest a rational approach to policy development, which usually involves a set of chronological steps that include problem identification, clarification of values, goals, and objectives, and identification of options to achieve goals, cost/benefit analysis of options, selection of a course of action, evaluation of the course of action, and modification to the program (p. 25).

Elements of Policy Development

Carley (1980) has suggested there are three elements to policy development, making political decisions about which values will be allocated, then rational determination through steps similar to those listed in the previous paragraph, and finally the need to recognize the bureaucratic structure will also affect the actual policy achieved.

Taylor et al. (1997) took umbrage with the rational notion of policy development and suggested that "in reality most policy is developed in a more disjointed, less rational and more political fashion" (p. 25). Their experience with policy-making has led them to believe that it is not possible to delineate and separate the elements so clearly:

> For example, one of us was involved in the development of a classification system for disadvantaged schools for a state department of education in Australia. We were required to utilise Australian Bureau of Statistics (ABS) data on a range of socio-economic measures to develop an index of disadvantage to classify schools so that

equity monies could be distributed to those schools serving the most disadvantaged communities. Supposedly, we were the "rational" experts employed to carry out the technical work after the political decision to initiate the Disadvantaged Schools Program had been made. What we very quickly found, however, was that the seemingly rational process of creating indices of disadvantage was fraught with political questions of which statistics would be used—income, occupation, educational levels, housing, Aboriginality, and so on—to measure disadvantage. Further, one index meant that certain schools would receive benefits which would be denied to other schools, while different indices derived from different components from the ABS had different effects. In the end we accepted an index which most closely confirmed the "expert" view of those who worked in the various regions of the State on the program, indicating very clearly the ongoing and interactive rational/political character of the policy development process. (p. 26)

There are multiple perspectives on how to develop policy and myriad ways to reach the policy product. We now examine a variety of approaches to suggest the range available.

Approaches to Policy Development

Clemmer (1991) suggested four approaches to policy development:

1. starting from scratch;
2. revising and updating existing policies;
3. fashioning new policies; and
4. adding or changing administrative regulations. (pp. 54–59)

In education policy-making, all four approaches are fairly common, but recently, with the advent of various reforms, many educators seem to be preoccupied with revising and updating existing policies. This is particularly true with respect to reforms of a governance nature such as consolidation of school boards. Current issues in need of policy development involve rights and recognition for LGBT and racialized students.

Let us look closer at each of the approaches identified by Clemmer (1991).

Starting from scratch

Starting policy development from scratch can be a lengthy and indeed onerous task. However, for practical purposes, it is suggested that basic policies be examined for how they were developed and then a blueprint articulated for the further development of policies. Such a blueprint will identify who has been charged with ensuring the policy gets developed, which stakeholders should be involved, what role these stakeholders should play, what the timeline for development should be, and what kind of implementation—widespread or pilot—is recommended.

It is imperative that adequate time be allowed for public review and discussion of draft policies. Stifling these processes will almost automatically guarantee their failure. Classroom teachers and building-level administrators may be highly critical of any policy they feel "imposed" on them because they were not given sufficient time for consultation and input. Considering that teachers and principals are the front-line implementers of most education policies, such a lack of foresight on the part of policy-makers can quickly kill any policy initiative.

Revising and updating existing policies

Over time, policies become outdated. People, communities, technologies, values, and priorities change, as do funding and governments. The revision and updating of existing policies is a normal aspect of policy-making. Clemmer (1991) offered this advice:

> in some cases it is harder to ferret out needed policy changes than
> it is to start from scratch. Most boards expect their superintendents
> and staff to constantly assess the effectiveness of current policies and
> regulations, and suggest needed policy changes or make desirable
> alterations in regulations. Though regular analysis of existing policies
> keeps revision at the level of "fine-tuning" and helps avoid the need
> for a major overhaul, new legislation or regulations at the national or
> state levels will often impose the need for drastic changes at the local
> level. (p. 57)

One suggestion is to establish a fixed date on which to trigger review or revision of a specific policy. For example, a newly developed policy might be scheduled for an automatic review every five years. Planned reviews keep policies current and up to date.

Align to context / audience

Fashioning new policies

Proactive leadership involves being on the leading edge of policy formulation, and educational leaders should always be on the alert for the need for new policies. Clemmer (1991) suggested that many policies are instituted because it is good practice to have them. That is, such policies let people know before anything happens how the board or the administration will likely act or react under a given set of circumstances (p. 58).

This approach to policy development assumes that the organization is familiar with the process and not necessarily starting from scratch. Organizations frequently adopt policies from other jurisdictions and fashion them to their particular situations or the local context.

Adding or changing administrative regulations

Actual policies are primarily concerned with values and principles; regulations are the nitty-gritty that spell out the actual ways and means of achieving or living up to those values and principles. Conditions under which policies operate will vary from time to time and hence there will be times when regulations demand revision.

Senior administration should be cognizant of this need for revision; the onus is on administration to recommend changes or additions to the board. These recommendations often become the actual changes to the regulation in question.

Policy Dissemination

The actual dissemination of a policy is sometimes overlooked in policy development. But this step matters. After all, if there is no effective mechanism for getting information on the new policy to those affected by it, then the process of policy development may have been for naught.

At the dissemination stage, it is imperative the policy-maker anticipate and evaluate a variety of factors before deciding on the appropriate course of action. Considerations such as the complexity of the policy changes, the degree to which the policy breaks with past tradition, the ability of personnel to enact the policy successfully, and the possible conflict of the policy with vested interests all need to be looked at carefully when an organization is deciding how to disseminate policy. This topic will be discussed in greater detail in chapter 8.

The Policy Development Cycle

An actual policy development cycle as suggested by First (1992) may be helpful in our discussion of this topic. As First stated, "policy development is continuous and overlapping. Various policies, problems, and domains will be in various steps of the cycle simultaneously" (p. 229). Each of these steps may include a variety of tasks, which will vary depending upon the particular policy area being addressed. Here is a summary of those steps:

Step 1: The need for attention to policy may arise in a variety of ways, from a Supreme Court ruling to a school revising an existing policy.

Step 2: As a result of a particular issue, concern, or problem being raised, staff review existing policies to determine which ones need attention.

Step 3: Information necessary for consideration of the problem in question is gathered. This step involves research and literature reviews in addition to consultations with as many sources as possible—teachers, consultants, parents, and others with interest and insights to share.

Step 4: When sufficient information has been gathered, someone (a committee, a consultant, a policy specialist) must study, deliberate, and determine the basic issues involved. Normally, a report with recommendations for the board's consideration will be prepared.

Step 5: The board receives the report. Ideally, meaningful discussion ensues and produces a consensus about the direction the policy will eventually take.

Step 6: The work of writing the first draft of the policy in question is assigned to staff or to a policy analyst or consultant.

Step 7: Before the first reading and subsequent deliberations at a board meeting, the public and those most affected by the proposed policy must have adequate notice that the policy is being considered. Time for public commentary is then provided on the agenda of a future board meeting.

Step 8: Revisions and rewriting take place in response to the board's deliberations.

Step 9: At a subsequent board meeting, there is a second reading of the proposed policy and time is provided for the public to give their input. The board may have further discussions as well.

Step 10: It is now time for final revision and for a careful review of the policy and its wording by legal counsel.

Step 11: At the time of the third reading at a board meeting, the board formally adopts the policy.

Step 12: The policy is then formally communicated to those immediately affected and the public at large.

Step 13: The policy is then implemented with plans for evaluation built into the implementation plan.

Step 14: The evaluation leads to revisions, updating, and improvement and eventually to restarting the policy development cycle. (pp. 229–231)

Although these steps appear to be straightforward and at first glance, perhaps simplistic and idealistic, we must realize that in the real world, the best laid plans of mice and men do not always go the way we would like. Policy development is a lengthy and at times, tedious process. Practicalities need to be kept in mind, but the cycle does give the student of policy a concise overview as to how such policy development is supposed to happen.

Concluding Comment

This chapter has given an overview of what is meant by policy development along with the various elements of and approaches to policy development. These approaches, together with the fourteen-step cycle, are highly practical and should be of considerable utility to those involved in policy development.

Chapter 6 examines the concept of policy implementation.

DISCUSSION/REFLECTION QUESTIONS

1. Policy development is sometimes described as being reactive. Is this an accurate characterization? Elaborate.

2. Clemmer (1991) says that policy development is "not a one-time activity" (p. 54). Have your personal experiences with policy development, if any, given you insight as to whether this is true?

3. Traditionally, how involved are teachers in policy development? Do teachers want to be involved in the process? Why or why not?

4. Do teachers perceive themselves as an integral part of the policy development process?

5. How practical and realistic are Clemmer's approaches to policy development?

6. How practical and realistic is First's (1992) fourteen-step policy development cycle?

7. Immediacy is sometimes a pressure on policy-making agencies. How can these agencies balance this pressure with the motivation to do a reasonable and credible job on developing a specific policy?

8. What other pressures might policy-making agencies face when attempting to develop policy? How might these pressures be managed?

6

Policy Implementation

Implementation Defined

It was Koenig's (1986) perception that "the great Achilles heel of the policy process is implementation" (p. 149). Educators generally concede that the other phases of policy-making, such as policy analysis and policy development, are less challenging than actually implementing the policy in question. Implementation is where the rubber hits the road or, as some educators would suggest, where theory hits practice.

Often viewed as the link between policy production and policy practice, implementation of policy occurs in a highly complex social environment; official policy agendas seldom intersect with local interests (Taylor et al., 1997). A long-debated question about implementation is the degree to which it should be spelled out in the actual policy. Sergiovanni et al. (1999) spoke to this concern:

> Individuals charged with putting a policy into effect often complain about overprescriptive language that leaves them little room to tailor the implementation to local conditions. They would rather have policy-makers sketch out the grand design and leave the details to them. Policy-makers, on the other hand, recognizing how easy it is to subvert some policies at the implementation stage, may be blatantly prescriptive if they suspect that those charged with implementing the policy are less than enthusiastic about it. State legislators, for example, may want to leave very little discretion to local school boards or superintendents regarding how statewide high school graduation requirements are to be interpreted and implemented. (pp. 232–233)

Pal (1997) referred to implementation as the "execution" of the developed policy (p. 145). He elaborated:

> Policy implementation is the stage of policy-making between the passage of a legislative act, the issuing of an executive order, the handing down of a judicial decision, or the promulgation of a regulatory rule, and the consequences of the policy for the people whom it affects. If the policy is inappropriate, if it cannot alleviate the problem for which it was designed, it will probably be a failure no matter how well it is implemented. (p. 146)

Policy implementation is indeed one of the most challenging aspects of policy-making. The key to implementation lies in the approach. The next section discusses a variety of possible approaches to implementation.

Approaches to Implementation

Colebatch (1998) suggested there are two basic approaches to policy implementation: a vertical perspective and a horizontal perspective. He had this to say about the vertical perspective:

> In the vertical perspective, implementation means that authorized decisions at the top coincide exactly with outcomes at the bottom: it is a question of securing compliance. This is the (usually tacit) assumption on which much of the writing on the question is based: that the policy process is best understood as the formulation of goals by "policy-makers," the selection of instruments to achieve them, and the assessment of the outcomes. This reflects constitutional models of government, and instrumental models of organization: it is seen as self-evident that those elected by the people to govern should be able to place their policies into action . . . . In the vertical dimension, the focus is on the policy goals, and people and organization come into the picture to the extent that they contribute (or obstruct) these goals. (p. 65)

By comparison, he commented that

> in the horizontal dimension, implementation is an exercise in collective negotiation: the focus shifts from the desired outcome to the process and the people through which it would be accomplished . . . . The horizontal dimension recognizes that policy is an ongoing process, and that the participants have their own agenda and therefore their own distinct perspective on any policy issue. (p. 65)

These approaches reflect distinct ideas about the concentration of power and control. They coincide with the top-down and bottom-up approaches articulated by Mazmanian, Sabatier, and Hjern (cited in Sabatier, 1993).

According to Mazmanian et al., the essential features of a top-down approach are that it begins with a policy decision by governmental officials and then asks these questions:

1. To what extent were the actions of implementing officials and target groups consistent with (the objectives and procedures outlined in) that policy decision?

2. To what extent were the objectives attained over time; i.e., to what extent were the impacts consistent with the objectives?

3. What were the principal factors affecting policy outputs and impacts, both those relevant to the official as well as other politically significant ones?

4. How was the policy reformulated over time on the basis of experience? (p. 267)

Hjern (1982) explained that the bottom-up approach starts by identifying the network of actors involved in service delivery in one or more local areas and asks them about their goals, strategies, activities, and contacts. It then uses the contacts as a vehicle to identify the local, regional, and national actors involved in the planning, financing, and execution of the relevant governmental and nongovernmental programs. This provides a mechanism for moving from street-level bureaucrats (the "bottom") to the "top" policy-makers in both the public and private sectors.

In her review of the literature on policy implementation, LaRocque (1983) listed three such models: the classical or technological model, the political model, and the cultural or evolutionary model. Musella (1989) offers the following descriptions of these models:

1. *Classical or technological model:* In this model, the relationship between policy-makers and policy implementers is assumed to be hierarchical, that of superordinate to subordinate. Thus, it is assumed that policy decisions at the superordinate level will be followed by implementation at the subordinate level. The role of the administrator is to ensure that policy change orders are carried out. Board policy, in conjunction with administrative and supervisory direction, leads directly to the implementation of changes.

2. *Political model:* In this model, the policy process is seen as a system of three environments, each with a specific function: policy formulation, policy implementation, and policy

evaluation. The relationship between policy-makers and policy implementers is assumed to be a balance of power, with each group having different resources under its control. Hence, cooperation between implementers and policy-makers must be negotiated.

3. *Cultural or evolutionary model:* In this model, policy is assumed to be a set of multiple dispositions to act, the realization of which depends both on the intrinsic qualities of the policy and on the characteristics of the setting for implementation. In this model, the administrator and the supervisor must understand the environment and the fit of the specific change to the environment at the time in question. This model can be applied to most policy changes, if we assume that the process leading to the change is as important as the process that follows the policy change. (pp. 96–97)

In practice, most policy implementation reflects a hybrid of approaches.

The following section examines a number of assumptions underlying policy implementation.

Underlying Assumptions of Policy Implementation

Downey (1988) suggested there are several assumptions to keep in mind when implementing education policy:

1. Educational institutions tend to be tradition oriented and resistant to change. Policies are future oriented and blueprints for change, so it is not surprising that they almost automatically generate negative reaction.

2. Educational organizations are staffed by well-trained professionals. Policies tend to be shaped, or at least authorized, by lay boards, so it is not surprising that they are almost automatically suspect.

3. Although most governing authorities realize that the process of public policy development must unfold in the context of community power and politics, they often forget that implementation must also unfold in that context. When the time for implementation arrives, internal politics and displays of power can thwart the process.

4. The implementation of new policies almost always calls for new commitments and extra expenditures of effort. Only under

certain conditions can such new commitments and efforts be
expected. (pp. 97–98)

Research Findings on Policy Implementation

Of all the aspects of policy, it is fair to say that policy implementation—or
rather successful policy implementation—presents the greatest challenge
to those working in the policy arena. We are therefore wise to consider
what the research on policy implementation is telling us. In one such
review of that literature on policy implementation research McLaughlin
(1991) offered the following summary of lessons:

1. The overarching, obvious conclusion running through empirical
   research on policy implementation is that it is incredibly hard to
   make something happen, most especially when one is working
   across layers of government and institutions. Issues requiring
   policy tend to be very complicated, and even when a policy is
   developed, there is no guarantee of its being successful.

2. Successful implementation generally requires a combination of
   pressure and support from policy (Elmore & McLaughlin, 1983;
   Fullan, 1986; McLaughlin & Pfeifer, 1988; Montjoy & O'Toole,
   1979; Zald & Jacobs, 1978). Both pressure and support seem to
   be in conflict with each other to some degree and require skillful
   negotiation in order to implement successfully.

3. Change is ultimately a problem of the smallest unit. At each
   point in the policy process, a policy is transformed as individuals
   interpret and respond to it. What is actually delivered or
   provided under the aegis of a policy depends finally on the
   individual at the end of the line—the "street-level bureaucrat"
   (Weatherley & Lipsky, 1977).

4. The environment is important for both individuals and their
   institutions. Because implementation takes place in an ever-
   changing setting, implementation problems are never solved.
   Rather, they evolve through a multistaged, iterative process.
   Every implementation action simultaneously changes policy
   problems, policy resources, and policy objectives (Majone &
   Wildavsky, 1977). New issues, new requirements, and new
   considerations emerge as the process unfolds. For example,
   the first challenge of implementation generally is to learn the
   rules of the game. What is supposed to be done? What are the
   legal requirements determining program activities? Clear goals,

well-specified statutes, and effective authority are important *external* policy variables at this initial stage (Elmore & McLaughlin, 1983; Sabatier & Mazmanian, 1980). Generally, it is only after these compliance concerns have been understood that implementers can move on to address issues of program development, the *quality* of implementation. At this stage, external factors recede in importance and internal factors such as commitment, motivation, and competence dominate.

5. There are few "slam bang" policy effects (McLaughlin, 1991, p. 175). This is because policy effects are necessarily indirect, operating through and within the existing setting. Thus, policy is transformed and adapted to conditions of the implementing unit. Consequently, local manifestation of state/province or federal policies will differ in fundamental respects and effective implementation may have different meanings in different settings. (pp. 187–190)

Policy implementation is a complicated process. It is perhaps the most challenging aspect of policy development. Those in organizations charged with policy implementation need a range of skill sets, including strong negotiating abilities and a keen understanding of human behavior and the change process.

In summary, McLaughlin (1991) offered the following insights:

Taken together, these lessons describe a model of implementation that moves from early notions of implementation as transmission or as a problem of incentives or authority to conceptions of implementation as bargaining and transformation (Ingram, 1977; Majone & Wildavsky, 1977; Ripley & Franklin, 1982, for example). This perspective on the implementation process highlights *individuals* rather than institutions and frames central implementation issues in terms of individual actor's incentives, beliefs, and capacity. Implementers at all levels of the system effectively negotiate their response, fitting their action to the multiple demands, priorities, and values of the policy itself. Further, this bargaining or negotiation is a continuous process, proceeding over time as policy resources, problems, and objectives evolve and are played against a dynamic institutional setting. This means that the nature of the bargain will change over time within settings and will most likely differ across units of the policy system. (p. 191)

Drawing on the work of a variety of policy researchers, Hogwood and Gunn (1997) suggested that perfect policy implementation is virtually

unattainable in practice. They listed several preconditions that would
have to be satisfied if perfect implementation were to be achieved:

1. *That the circumstances external to the implementing agency do not
   impose crippling constraints.* Some obstacles to implementation
   are outside the control of administrators because they are
   external to the policy and the implementing agency. Some of
   these obstacles might be physical or political; there is very little,
   if anything, administrators can do to overcome them except in
   their capacity as advisers, by ensuring that such possibilities are
   kept in mind during the policy-making stage.

2. *That adequate time and sufficient resources are made available to
   the program.* Policies that are physically or politically feasible
   may still fail to achieve stated intentions. A common reason is
   that too much is expected too soon, especially when attitudes
   or behavior are involved (as in, for example, attempts to alter
   discriminatory attitudes toward the LGBT community or to
   recognize reconciliation issues for First Nations students).
   Another reason is that politicians will sometimes fund the
   policy "end" but not the "means," so that expenditure restrictions
   may starve a statutory program of adequate resources.

3. *That the required combination of resources is actually available.*
   There must not only be constraints in terms of overall
   resources but also the appropriate combination of resources
   must be available at each stage in the implementation process.
   A bottleneck often occurs when, for example, money, human
   resources, land, equipment, and building materials must come
   together to construct a new school in an economically depressed
   area; if one or more of these resources is delayed, the project as a
   whole is set back by several months.

4. *That the policy to be implemented is based upon a valid theory
   of cause and effect.* Policies are sometimes ineffective not
   because they are badly implemented, but because they are bad
   policies. That is, the policy may be based upon an inadequate
   understanding of a problem to be solved, its causes and cure,
   or of an opportunity, its nature, and what is needed to exploit
   it. Pressman and Wildavsky (1973) describe any policy as
   a "hypothesis containing initial conditions and predicted
   consequences" (p. 240). That is, the typical reasoning of
   the policy-maker is along the lines of "if X is done at time

t(1) then Y will result at time t(2)" (p. 240). Every policy incorporates a theory of cause and effect (normally unstated in practice). If the policy fails, the underlying theory may be at fault rather than the execution of the policy.

5. *That the relationship between cause and effect is direct and that there are few, if any, intervening links.* Pressman and Wildavsky (1973) argue that policies that depend on a long sequence of cause-and-effect relationships are particularly liable to break down since "the longer the chain of causality, the more numerous the reciprocal relationships among the links and the more complex implementation becomes" (p. 241). In other words, the more links in the chain, the greater the risk that some of them will fail—that is, prove to be poorly conceived or badly executed.

6. *That dependency relationships are minimal.* Perfect implementation requires a single implementing agency that need not depend on other agencies for success; or, if other agencies must be involved, that dependency relationships are minimal in number and importance. Where implementation requires not only a complex series of events and linkages but also agreement at each event among a large number of participants—as is often the case in practice—then the probability of a successful or even a predictable outcome is further reduced.

7. *That there is understanding of, and agreement on, objectives.* There should be complete understanding of, and agreement on, the objectives to be achieved. This condition should persist throughout the implementation process.

8. *That tasks are fully specified in complete detail and correct sequence.* The difficulty of achieving this condition of perfect implementation is obvious. It is desirable, and generally inevitable, that there be some room for discretion and improvisation in even the most carefully planned program.

9. *That there is perfect communication and coordination.* There must be perfect communication among and coordination of the various elements or agencies involved in the program. Even as we claim that perfect coordination is necessary, the reality is that such coordination is all but impossible. Communication has an important contribution to make to coordination and to implementation generally. However, perfect communication is

as unattainable a condition as are most of the others that have been discussed.

10. *That those in authority can demand and obtain perfect compliance.* The final and perhaps least attainable condition of perfect implementation is that those in authority are also those in power and that they are able to secure total and immediate compliance from others (both internal and external to the agency) whose consent and cooperation are required for the success of the program. The reality is that there may be conflicts between departments and agencies, and those with the formal authority to demand cooperation may lack the power to back up those demands or the will to exercise them. (pp. 238–245)

Suffice to say, there is no perfect implementation of policy. That said, policy-makers are well advised to ensure that, within reason, as many of the preconditions articulated here be in place as possible.

With that point in mind, we move on to discussing various guidelines that have been suggested for effective implementation.

Guidelines for Effective Implementation

Downey (1988) suggested the following guidelines that, although not guaranteeing perfect implementation, may facilitate varying degrees of successful or effective implementation:

1. The earlier staff members are involved in the policy-making process, the more likely they are to develop commitment to the policy and willingness to expend energy in its implementation.

2. The more precisely patterns of participation are planned and incorporated into the system's policies on policy-making, the more effective involvement will be in its dual purpose of enhancing the policy-making capability and of developing commitment to enacted policies.

3. The less a governing authority is required (or inclined) to flaunt its powers of policy-making, the more likely it is to receive the cooperation of its staff.

4. The less a governing authority and its executives are willing to exercise authority when it is needed, the more likely they are to lose the respect of staff and the ability to exercise leadership.

5. For a governing authority and its executives, assuming that the participatory mode of policy-making requires less in the way

of coordination and facilitation of staff effort invites chaos in procedures and wastes of staff time and effort. (p. 101)

Concluding Comment

This chapter has examined the plethora of challenges to successful policy implementation: specifically, what is meant by implementation was discussed along with several approaches or models of policy implementation. In an effort to prevent policy-makers from reinventing the wheel, I have given considerable attention to research findings on implementation. From those research findings emanate several strategies to assist the policy-maker in what has been described as the trickiest phase of policy.

Chapter 7 looks at policy evaluation.

DISCUSSION/REFLECTION QUESTIONS

1. Colebatch (1998) spoke about policy being implemented from either a vertical perspective or from a horizontal perspective. Sabatier and Mazmanian (1980) promoted the top-down approach, and Hjern (1982) advocated a bottom-up approach. What approach or approaches have you personally experienced when a policy or policies have been implemented? Which might work better and why?

2. Various policy researchers have suggested that perfect implementation is unattainable. Do you think this is a valid assumption? Why or why not?

3. Do educators as a group want to be involved in the implementation policy? Why or why not? Elaborate.

4. What might you see as the most significant impediment(s) to policy implementation? Elaborate.

5. Comment on how you might confront or overcome a significant impediment to policy implementation.

7

Policy Evaluation

Policy evaluation should be an obvious aspect of any form of policy development. Evaluation, as suggested by Downey (1988), is a process of determining the effectiveness and efficiency of policies to ascertain whether or not they have achieved their goals and intents. As Colebatch (1998) has stated,

> evaluation completes the [policy-making] cycle; it enables policy-makers to know to what extent they are achieving their objectives, and to act accordingly. The common sense of evaluation is clear: if policy is concerned with achieving goals, then it is only sensible to check whether or not these have been attained. Managers want to be able to show that their programmes are effective. (p. 67)

Fowler (2009) commented that evaluation is a form of applied research designed to determine if a policy works the way it was intended to work. In today's organizations, there seems to be a proliferation of policies. Whether this multitude of policies is necessary and effective can be determined only if a methodical plan is put into place to evaluate their effectiveness.

The Political Nature of Evaluation

While acknowledging the importance of evaluation, Pal (1997) commented on the highly political nature of the process:

> Consult any text on policy analysis and you will find passages extolling the indispensability of program evaluation. It could hardly be otherwise, given that program evaluation is primarily about trying to figure out how successful a policy has been, whether it met its objectives, how far it fell short, and what might be done to improve its impact. The same passages that extol evaluation, however, are usually

complemented by ones that say that it is expensive, difficult, rarely conclusive, and politically unpopular. Precisely because evaluation is so potentially crucial to the fortunes of a policy or program, opponents and supporters work hard to get the evaluation results they need to strengthen their case. That is, if evaluation takes place at all. Not only is it politically sensitive (who wants to hear bad news?), it can seem secondary to the really important job of designing and implementing solutions to public problems. Policy evaluation therefore has enjoyed more theoretical than practical popularity, and in Canada at least, has not been enthusiastically supported either as a government or a third party (i.e., foundations or think tanks) activity. This is changing. The new emphasis on results, coupled with a gradual shift to special operating agencies, contracted-out services, and partnerships, increases the need for evaluation because it puts new pressures on governments to be accountable. (p. 233)

Pal's comments trigger a number of salient questions. Who does the evaluation—the same people who develop and who implement the policy? If that is the case, one could argue that there is indeed a serious conflict of interest. An example that comes to mind, albeit a tad ridiculous, might be a police officer who commits a crime and whose own police organization does the investigation into that crime. In reality we know that, in most cases, an outside police organization is called in to investigate. But that organization is still a *police* organization, so maybe my example is not so ridiculous after all. Who should do the actual policy evaluation is not an easy question to answer.

Another question might be whether the organization developing the policy avoids evaluating the policy for fear of what shortcomings that evaluation might reveal. This is food for thought indeed as we look at the importance of evaluation.

Significance of Evaluation

Koenig (1986) emphasized the significance of evaluation to the policy-making process:

> The availability of competently conducted and genuinely considered evaluation constitutes a critical juncture in democratic policy-making. Without a network of external evaluations, policy-making is not systematically reviewed and assessed but drones on in privacy, free to commit error and to expend resources profligately. Without competent evaluations, higher executives, legislatures and the citizenry will remain ignorant of the actual performance of policy-makers and implementers, and will lose their democratic birthright to judge, reward, and punish those who engage in policy acts, subject to their approval. (p. 183)

Evaluation of all policies should be an ongoing part of the policy development process, but as Clemmer (1991) suggested, "it is especially important with new policies or recent revisions, or in cases where enforcement is especially difficult" (p. 187). He also made the following suggestion:

> One of the best evaluative questions asks members of the policy's "beneficiaries" if the policy is having its intended effect. Of course this presupposes a policy with a purpose, which ought to be a fair assumption. If, for example, the policy was designed to allow pupils more after-school help with classwork, the evaluator will want to know if children are in fact getting more help or if the help being received is in a form that is useful to the pupils. Do the regulations impose unnecessary restrictions in some schools that have always provided extra help for pupils but not during the precise hours prescribed by the regulations? If so, perhaps the principal or the superintendent ought to allow more flexibility. (pp. 187–188)

Sergiovanni et al. (1999) suggested that policy evaluation often calls for trained policy evaluators to find out what the policy change has accomplished and how people feel about it. The reality, they said, is that without formal evaluation, policy change will be reflected by people in the system saying things such as "This sure beats the way we used to do it!" or "I knew this wouldn't work!" (p. 233).

Criteria for Effective Policies

Keeping in mind the practicality that Sergiovanni et al. (1999) referred to, we can draw from the criteria put forth by various authors when we evaluate policy. Clemmer (1991) offered the following criteria for our consideration:

1. *Pertinent:* Only policies on applicable topics deserve development time.
2. *Timely:* Policies should respond to actual needs, but should not be enacted until essential facts are known.
3. *Functional:* Policy should make possible that which needs to be done.
4. *Practicable:* If a policy cannot be implemented, do not adopt it. (pp. 104–105)

He followed up these criteria with this general commentary:

> Although good policies allow for a reasonable measure of interpretation, they are stated in language specific enough that they provide real guidance. Good policies treat broad, general issues that have long-term implications; poor policies often respond to specific incidents and prescribe narrow judgments, and they often prove unenforceable.

Unlike those fostered in a business, where profit is an abiding incentive, a school district's policies should enhance the achievement of its own goals, which are educational or service-oriented. Of course, if a policy is prescribed by a certain law, it should faithfully adhere to legislative intent, as interpreted by the state's attorney general or the courts. (p. 105)

Good policies should enable organizations—especially schools, whose primary mission is to educate students—to be productive and law-abiding members of society. Unfortunately, sometimes laws (e.g., those that discriminate against some of the most vulnerable members of our society) do have a negative effect on policies, and policy-makers are often at a loss with how to deal with such restrictiveness.

Clemmer (1991) listed several questions that could be used in the evaluation process:

1. Is the policy within the board's legal and moral areas of interest, authority, and responsibility?
2. Does the policy express the district's values or intentions?
3. Is the policy statement general rather than specific?
4. Does the policy respond to a common set of circumstances?
5. Does the policy avoid making the board appear arbitrary or capricious?
6. Does the policy tell you who is affected by its implementation?
7. Does the policy tell you when it should be applied?
8. Does the policy conform to the normal appeal procedure?
9. Does the policy comply with existing policy or law?
10. Is the policy the result of local effort and not an "import"?
11. Does the policy reflect broad and deliberate discussion?
12. Can the policy's effectiveness be evaluated?
13. Is the policy educationally sound?
14. Exactly what is authorized or required by the policy? (p. 106)

Characteristics of Good Policies

According to Clemmer (1991), good policies allow for a reasonable measure of interpretation. At the same time, they are stated in language specific enough that they provide real guidance. One of the consistent criticisms of policy is that a policy may be restrictive, depending on its wording. Clemmer's point is valuable because in education, we deal with individuals and their complexities daily. Very few issues are black and white;

rather, situations tend to be gray. It is incumbent upon those involved in developing education policy to be cognizant of these complexities and to word policy in such a way as to allow for flexibility in dealing with the myriad issues educators face every day.

Another characteristic suggested by Clemmer (1991) is that for policies to be effective, they should remain consistent with other local policies. There may be older policies still on the books that will have to be removed to ensure this consistency. Current and up-to-date are also hallmarks of good policies, according to Clemmer (p. 105). Although this point may appear to be common sense, it bears mentioning here. Lastly, he suggested that sound policies are proactive and reflect the personality of the organization they represent.

Types of Evaluation Studies

The following types of studies for evaluating policy were suggested by Koenig (1986): policy outputs, policy impact or performance, goal achievement, program processes evaluation, and benefit–cost and cost-effectiveness methodologies:

1. *Policy outputs:* These encompass the tangible and symbolic manifestations of public policy, which are the observable indicators of what a government agency or program does. While this information is useful, however, it tells little about the quality and the effects of the actual policy's performance and consequently may not be all that helpful in the evaluation process.

2. *Policy impact or performance:* These examine the extent to which a policy output has accomplished its assigned goals. Impact evaluation focuses on the delineation of operationally defined goals, the criteria of success, and the measurement of progress toward goals. Implicit in impact evaluation are questions of causality: has a policy or program produced a change in the target population in the direction and to the degree that policymakers intended?

3. *Goal achievement:* This is a more intensive variant of impact evaluation: have the goals of a policy or program been achieved? Evaluation research employs objective, systematic methods to assess the extent to which the goals are realized and examines the factors underlying success and failure. This task becomes complicated, sometimes hopelessly so, when the political process by which goals are created leaves them in a murky

state. Evaluating programs according to goal achievement becomes complex if some goals are attained more than others and if the goals are interrelated. A goal-achievement evaluation faces difficulties in fulfilling a common function of evaluations: enhancing the quality of future program activities. Many participants are involved in determining goals, in allocating resources to achieve them, and in structuring and restructuring operations. If an evaluation illuminates ways to improve performance, securing their adoption becomes an enormous political task. Groups such as school boards, their respective committees, and school building administrative teams all have shared interests in preserving the status quo. Greater efficiency, through adoption of changes illuminated by evaluation studies, becomes less desirable when it is compared to the already established largess, and even worse, by threatening its continuation. Not surprisingly, goal evaluations have poor track records in leading to more effective programs. They are also bedeviled by an image of irrelevance in the eyes of those who logically should be most inclined to use them. Program managers who oversee the activities on which evaluations concentrate typically find evaluations largely unresponsive to their information needs and commonly dismiss them as too slow, too inconclusive, and too prone to answer the wrong questions.

4. *Program processes evaluation:* This method centers on specific steps in an agency's work and performance, internal dynamics and actual operations to understand a program's strengths and weaknesses. It examines why certain things are happening, how a program's parts fit together, and how others (clients, legislators, executives) perceive the program. This evaluation emphasizes how a product is produced rather than the product itself. Process evaluation can light the way to better decision-making, improved procedures, more efficient funding, and more productive program design.

5. *Benefit–cost and cost-effectiveness methodologies:* These apply the test of efficiency in evaluating program expenditures, emphasizing measurable costs and benefits. Costs and benefits are identified and measured, the balance between them is determined, and programs are judged according to their ability to generate more benefits than costs. This approach often ignores

nonquantifiable factors, however, the importance of which can render evaluation useless, if not dangerous. In social programs, which abound with nonquantifiable elements, the tendency is to over-stress their measurable features. Generally, program costs lend themselves more readily to quantification than program benefits. (pp. 191–193)

As with other categorizations, the types of evaluation studies discussed in this chapter (and in academic literature generally) seem linear in nature. In practice, however, these types commonly overlap and seldom exist in isolation. Once again, the word *hybrid* seems to be a relevant feature of such categorizations.

Concluding Comment

This chapter has provided an overview of what evaluation entails with a particular emphasis on what constitutes good and effective policies. Various types of evaluation studies were also discussed. Having considered what has been said by policy experts, we might suspect that, without evaluation, policy remains impotent. Although there are many evaluation techniques in vogue, the best methods to use depend on the particular sector and the intention of a specific policy.

Chapter 8 considers the challenges presented in policy dissemination.

DISCUSSION/REFLECTION QUESTIONS

1. How significant is policy evaluation to the policy-making process?

2. In your experience, how political has policy evaluation been?

3. What questions would you ask if you were assigned to evaluate a new policy (student supervision, for example)?

4. Who should be involved in policy evaluation and why?

5. Comment on your perceptions of the following stakeholders' roles in policy evaluation: teacher, school administrator, parent, school board trustee, school superintendent.

6. Do you observe policy evaluation happening in various organizations such as schools and school boards? Elaborate.

7. What might be an impediment(s) to policy evaluation?

8. How might you overcome an impediment(s) to policy evaluation? Elaborate.

8

Policy Dissemination

Defining Policy Dissemination

Policy dissemination differs from implementation in that dissemination refers to the process of making the various stakeholders aware of and informed about the policy in question. In fact, this is a vital aspect of the policy process because those intimately involved with a policy's implementation must understand the intricacies of the policy; otherwise, the policy is probably doomed to be ineffective. This is indeed a challenge in its own right, so the question of how dissemination should occur requires significant consideration.

Clemmer (1991) brought the question of dissemination down to a very practical level:

> Because relatively few persons may have assisted in the development of a particular policy, unless it is controversial and has attracted public attention the vast majority of . . . students, employees, and patrons will most likely be unaware of its existence or its implications. All major district players should be informed about the new policy and how it will be administered, but the audience of first magnitude is always the one comprised of the persons most *affected* by the policy. (p. 186)

Scheirer and Griffith (1990) characterized dissemination as "the initial diffusion of information about the program [policy] among potential users" (p. 164). The quality of this information and how it is conveyed to potential users of the policy are very significant because these factors help to determine whether a policy will succeed. The information disseminated should be constructed in such a way as to be easily understood by those for whom it is intended, and the dissemination should be well planned and comprehensive. One obvious method of dissemination in our increasingly digital society is the use of social media alongside the traditional forms of print, radio, and television. Social media has a big advantage over traditional media because it operates at a fraction of the cost and can have wide and rapid reach.

Acknowledging the tacit assumption of "universal acceptance of dissemination" (Knott and Wildavsky (1991, p. 214) reminded us that we should not take universal acceptance at face value. In their words,

> the chorus of acclaim should be enough to warn us that the term may be vacuous, a convenient excuse for failures that may be attributed to the lack of this essential ingredient, whatever it is supposed to be . . . . Are there no conditions under which dissemination might be counter-productive, the less done, the better? The interests of senders may not necessarily coincide with those of receivers. (p. 214)

When new policies are complex or involve new ways of behavior among institutional members, it may be necessary to lay the groundwork for such changes through conferences and discussions in addition to the more formal channels of communication (Rich, 1974). Rich offered this advice to the policy-maker:

> the policy-maker must anticipate and evaluate a host of factors prior to deciding on the proper course of action; such factors as the complexity of the policy changes, the degree to which the policy breaks with past practices, the ability of personnel to execute the policy successfully, and the possible conflict of the policy with vested interests are all matters that merit careful assessment in determining dissemination procedures. (p. 31)

When one is involved in aspects of policy-making such as dissemination, it is easy to become entangled in what I refer to as "not being able to see the forest for the trees" syndrome. By this I mean that those directly involved in policy-making are so caught up with the intricacies of policy that they may lack a certain objectivity when it comes to looking at the policy-making process with a critical lens. We tend to look at objectivity as being negative, yet objectivity should contribute to a better policy product because of the issues and concerns articulated and (one hopes) addressed before the final policy is developed. There should be abundant opportunities for discussion about the possible implications of policy; as organizational theory suggests, the more people involved in these discussions who may be affected by a specific policy, the better the policy process should be.

Concluding Comment

This chapter has underscored the importance of dissemination. Although dissemination is closely linked to implementation, there are important differences. Successful dissemination is key to successful implementation. The policy-making process is complicated and all too often, dissemination is taken for granted. This is particularly true of education policy-making, where time is an especially rare and precious commodity. We recognize that people are not always receptive to policy communication, especially if policy implementation requires in-service training or professional development, but the onus is on those in leadership positions, both at the building and district levels, to ensure that dissemination is given the attention it warrants.

Chapter 9 examines the differences between policy and regulations.

DISCUSSION/REFLECTION QUESTIONS

1. How significant, in your opinion, is policy dissemination?

2. Suggest several dissemination strategies that could facilitate the successful implementation of education policy at the school level and then at the district level.

3. In your experience, how much attention has been paid to policy dissemination? What consequences have you observed?

4. What problems have you experienced with the dissemination process? How may these problems have been overcome?

5. What impact has the Internet had on policy dissemination? What impact has social media in particular had on policy dissemination?

9

Policy and Regulations

As we discussed earlier, policies serve as general guidelines. Policy refers to what needs to be done; regulation refers to how it gets done (Clemmer, 1991). Clemmer further clarified:

> Whereas policies are designed as guides for discretionary action, regulations are formulated for the express purpose of delimiting the range of discretionary choices. Some regulations are stricter than others, but most include more verbs like *must, shall,* and *will* than do policies, in which *may* and *should* tend to be more prevalent. (p. 182)

Policy specifics—sometimes referred to as the nuts and bolts of a policy—are covered in the regulations. Although there may be examples of policy that do not require regulations, more often than not, regulations are required to ensure the effective implementation of the policy.

Several writers on policy use the term *procedures* instead of regulations. In this book, both terms are used interchangeably.

Questions for Consideration

Clemmer (1991) listed several questions that should be considered in the development of education policy regulations or procedures:

1. Exactly what does the board want this policy to do?
2. What results will demonstrate that the policy is achieving the board's intent?
3. What does the policy require, permit, or prohibit?
4. Are there laws or contracts that must be taken into account?
5. Will these regulations apply to the entire school system or only to one subdivision (e.g., school, class, grade)?

6. Would it be advisable to have the board approve these
   regulations?
7. Are these regulations too lenient or too strict?
8. What is the worst that can be said about these regulations?
9. What defense can be raised against these objections?
10. Am I willing to modify these regulations if they prove
    inappropriate? (p. 183)

It is obvious that these questions are basic and practical, characteristics highly valuable to the policy-making process. Weighing the answers to these questions pragmatically when policy regulations are being formed and refined may yield a set of regulations that is both realistic and workable.

Suggestions for the Writing of Regulations

Clemmer (1991) also offered the following suggestions as guidelines for writers of effective regulations:

1. Keep the regulations as simple, concise, and clear as possible.
   Avoid moralizing or preaching.
2. Be sure the target of the regulations is clearly spelled out.
   Determine who needs to care about what the regulations say.
3. Be succinct and define important terms. Never assume that
   everyone will automatically know what you mean.
4. Use the present tense wherever possible. The future and the past
   are not a part of the here-and-now.
5. Do not be afraid to use imperative language (pupils *will*,
   teachers *shall*, principals *must*).
6. Say the most important things first. Start with the concrete and
   move to the abstract, as effective teachers do.
7. Use simple sentences. Complex sentences or requirements easily
   become confusing and counterproductive.
8. Note exceptions to one sentence in the very next sentence.
   People who need information quickly do not read footnotes.
9. Check your regulations for clarity. Have someone not
   acquainted with the policy or the problem read each draft.
10. Be certain your regulations acknowledge the rights of all parties
    in the regulatory process. Foremost among these rights is the
    assurance of substantive due process.

11. If in doubt, have an attorney check the language of your regulations for legal implications. Good regulations should prevent litigation, not precipitate it. (pp. 184–185)

The regulations associated with any policy are important because they represent the practical application of that policy. The guidelines outlined here are straightforward and easy to understand. Obviously, Clemmer exemplifies the theme of his guidelines—that is, he practices what he preaches.

The Policy Manual

One challenge of school administrators is to keep their heads above the continuous flow of communication that enters their worlds daily; keeping everything in order and easily accessible is not an easy task. In the past, administrators were encouraged to create a policy manual or handbook in hard copy to ensure all policies (with their attendant regulations and procedures) were readily available. This manual would be a constant work in progress or, to use a contemporary term, "fluid": it would never be final and complete because policies and regulations are continually being revised and updated. For reasons of practicality, paper policy manuals were produced in three-ring binders to permit quick replacement of various pages.

Fast-forward to the age of computer technology and the Internet. Those three-ring binder manuals have become relics, and policies have a convenient home on school and school board websites. The flexibility of websites has made the updating of policies and regulations a relatively simple task. However, the retrieval of policies and regulations from these websites by "consumers" interested in learning about a specific policy is not always so simple.

I recently visited the websites of twelve Canadian school districts to check how they handled the storage of policies. I came away from that exercise feeling somewhat frustrated. Only two of the websites had *Policies* as a major heading on the home page. These websites were indeed excellent as they contained comprehensive information about their policies and the information was organized conveniently for the layperson. Using the search function on each of these websites allowed me to find information on school districts' policies in almost all the remaining school districts. I strongly suggest all school districts use the heading *Policies* in the design of their websites; doing so would certainly facilitate anyone's efforts to familiarize himself or herself with the specific policies of a particular agency. (Note, however, that several district websites use the term *Administrative Procedures* to present policies and regulations.)

The importance of the policy manual, whether it be hard copy or digital, cannot be overstated. As First (1992) commented,

> the policy manual . . . should be a living document that serves as the chief guide for . . . management and, therefore, is a signpost for administrators, board members, teachers, and other staff who are responsible for carrying out their duties. Unfortunately, in today's legalistic world, policy manuals have become far thicker and wordier than they should be, but still they are very necessary and important enough that a district [or school] should make time and resources available to do a good job on the initial and subsequent updates. (p. 237)

It is an understatement to say that we are now living in a digital world. Policies are no exception: they too live in the digital world, specifically on school and school board websites. One major advantage to this new location is accessibility; even the layperson with very basic knowledge of computers is able to locate policies on various subjects just by pressing a few keys. One could not have accessed the principal's policy manual on his or her office shelf so easily! But there are disadvantages to accessibility, too. Recall the points I mentioned earlier about the role of the Internet in disseminating policy.

This chapter has concentrated on the writing of policy regulations. Computers and the Internet facilitate policy-makers' examining of policy regulations from other jurisdictions; these efforts should result in better written regulations. Suffice to say that policy-making and its various aspects have taken a giant leap forward as a result of computerization.

Concluding Comment

Regulations or procedures play a significant role in the policy process. This chapter has offered several practical suggestions for facilitating the writing of policy regulations and for making those regulations accessible to the people directly affected by these policies, including members of the general public. Not to be underemphasized is the importance of the policy manual or handbook, now made much more conveniently accessible via the Internet to all those interested in policy. Its digital existence is a real time saver for busy teachers and school administrators.

The role of research in policy-making is discussed in chapter 10.

DISCUSSION/REFLECTION QUESTIONS

1. Comment on your perceptions of the terms policies, regulations, and procedures.

2. Policies and regulations may be more commonly associated with school boards rather than school buildings. Is this an accurate association? Why or why not?

3. What factor(s) may impede the formal development of regulations/procedures at the school level? What suggestions would you make to help ameliorate this situation?

4. How has the Internet facilitated/impeded the development of policy regulations and procedures? Elaborate.

5. From school to school, and from school district to school district, do you perceive that there is much sharing or indeed collaboration when it comes to developing policy regulations/procedures? Elaborate.

10

The Role of Research in Policy-Making

What is the relationship between research and policy-making? Does research influence policy-making? Graduate students in particular might assume a close relationship between policy and research, yet that is not what researchers find.

The Significance of Research

According to Berliner (1990), "research, unfortunately, either does not influence educational policy or influences it very slowly" (p. 263). He went on to explain why this was so:

> First, policy in the educational arena influences large numbers of people who think that by virtue of having gone to school that they have informed opinions. Unlike, say, space policy, timber clearing policy, or rate setting policies for interstate commerce, educational policy is intertwined with the daily lives of people at the local level. More than in other areas of policy-making, educational policies often appear tied to the emotions, politics, social relationships, and fiscal interests of a local, vocal and broad-based constituency. When policy is made under such conditions, research ordinarily has a minor role to play. A second reason that research often fails to inform policy is that in many areas of intense public debate educational research has, until recently, been lacking or uninformative. (p. 263)

Clune (1993) had this to say:

> The importance of educational research is underestimated because much research is not useful, and much of the research that is useful shows that many educational practices are ineffective. But research findings about effective practices are gradually accumulating, and

these tend to be quickly seized upon by a policy system that is hungry for solutions. Finding out how to increase educational achievement is a difficult task for everyone, including policy-makers and practitioners; good research is needed to establish new directions. (p. 127)

Loveless (1998) elaborated on the perceived impotence of educational research:

At its current stage of intellectual history, then, educational research is in a tenuous position, both in terms of its reputation as a disciplinary field within the academy and in terms of its standing as a body of verifiable knowledge. This state of affairs has important ramifications for the use of research findings in the real world. Research can offer only ambiguous direction to policy. The importance of this ambiguity is magnified because, with the traditional routes to academic prestige closed off, educational research must hunt elsewhere for legitimation. Policy-making forums are good places to look. The transaction that is offered to policy-makers is research for legitimacy. Researchers' reputations are enhanced when their ideas are realized in legislation or regulation. In return, policy-makers are able to claim that their initiatives reflect "what the research says" and they gain a stamp of scientific approval (even if quasi-scientific) for the causes they champion. These transactions are particularly powerful when it comes to educational reform since decision-makers routinely embrace findings that have not been tested or confirmed by practical application in classrooms. Compounding the error, when such findings are converted into substantive policy proposals, the ambiguities of research may be stripped away and forgotten. (pp. 282–283)

In a similar vein, Finn (1991) took a pessimistic view on how educational research has affected policy:

To put it simply, our labors haven't produced enough findings that Americans can use or even see the use of. Over the past two decades, there has been a goodly amount of systematic inquiry and a flood of studies, reports, and recommendations, yet our education system has by many measures worsened. I do not say that research has caused the decline, only that it has failed to counteract it. Education research has not fulfilled its role in the effort to improve our schools, perhaps because it runs into much skepticism from practitioners and policy- makers. Hence, its effects are limited, and this in turn fosters skepticism as to its potential—a wicked cycle. (p. 39)

I tend to conduct research that is highly pragmatic and (I hope!) of considerable utility to educators in schools and school board offices. I am not opposed to educational research of an esoteric nature, but having been a high school teacher and a high school principal for many years in my earlier life, I tend to situate myself in the context of a practitioner—hence the pragmatism in my research agenda. Perhaps I am also motivated by the fact that faculties of education are continually being criticized for their lack of utility and practicality in their bachelor's and master's degrees. My objective is to counteract such criticism by doing the kind of research I do. And with that thought, we shall segue into the next section, which deals with why we should conduct policy research.

Why Conduct Policy Research?

Ozga (2000) advanced several arguments for policy research in education. She pointed out that education research should not be confined to the useful or to knowledge that improves pupil performance. She contends that "research should be useful, but usefulness is not a straightforward concept, and enhancing pupil performance, while desirable, is not a sufficient description of the proper and legitimate concerns of education research" (p. 5). She continues:

> Teachers should engage in research, where possible and appropriate, in partnership with, and supported by higher education institutions. All teachers should be encouraged to feel themselves members of a research community, and should be enabled to participate in research debates, and to develop an orientation towards research and enquiry that carries into their professional practice. (p. 5)

That is, teachers in all sectors should be active in and even lead policy research because of its capacity to inform their own policy directions and to encourage autonomous, critical judgement of government policy.

O'Reilly (1991) had this to say about the need for good education policy research:

> Fundamentally, we require good policy research to link the dominant national and provincial policies of state and governance to emerging changing views of the nature of learning, of education, of school, of organization, and of management. At the same time, we cannot allow corporatist, managerial policies, structures and relationships to be applied unthinkingly to education. Educational policies, structures and relationships must be embedded in the nature of education itself and in our beliefs of the nature of learning, of teaching and of child and youth development. (p. 5)

Cohen and Garet (1991) concluded that "there is plenty of evidence that research affects policy, but generally this seems to happen in odd and unexpected ways" (p. 135). Specifically, they viewed most policy research, at least in education, as tending to influence the broad assumptions and beliefs underlying policies, not particular decisions. They further stated:

> Better methodology and policy relevance in applied research in education have not produced more convergent findings. This is in part because most policy-oriented research concerns programs with broad and conflicting aims, but it is also attributable to methodological conflict among research approaches and to the fact that the advance of applied research tends to complicate and redefine issues. As a result, improving applied research does not tend to produce more authoritative advice about social policy. (pp. 135–136)

I appreciate the differing perspectives presented but do take some umbrage with the comment from Ozga (2000) that education research not be confined to the useful or the applied. When we are discussing whether educational research has an effect on policy, the risk is that the more esoteric educational research becomes, the less impact it will have on education policy—and if we take that perspective to its logical conclusion, the less impact education policy will have on practice in classrooms and in schools.

On a More Optimistic Note

Whether pragmatism should trump esotericism in educational research is a debate that will not go away anytime soon. There is, however, commentary in the literature that speaks "to the ambiguity of purposes and the challenges of methods and communication in increasing the utilization of policy research" (Heck, 2004, p. 22). Notwithstanding this perspective, Heck (2004) acknowledged the inherent value of policy research:

> Lest the reader despair about even attempting to do policy research, although the direct influence of policy studies on making particular policy decisions has been modest, the indirect influence on policy-making has been more significant, due to the role policy research has had in sharpening and reformulating policy issues and sometimes leading to new strategies for approaching social problems (Boyd, 1988). Although policymakers may not routinely act based on the results of a particular research study, studies of their behavior suggest that they do assimilate information, concepts, generalizations, and perspectives from a variety of sources including research that shape their understandings (Lindblom & Cohen, 1979; Weiss, 1982, 1991). (p. 22)

Similarly, Berliner (1990) expressed guarded optimism regarding the relationship between policy-making and research:

> The difficulty in setting and enforcing policy in education merely makes the task difficult, not impossible. As the research community in education grows and respect for the findings, concepts, theories, and technology that it yields also grows, we can expect more informed debates about educational policy. But the social, political, philosophical and fiscal issues that policy-makers must attend to always exert great influence on their decisions. Research must, therefore, be seen as just one of the many sources of information and beliefs from which policy is derived. We probably cannot improve much on our ranking in the set of concerns that policy-makers must consider. But we can improve on the quality and usefulness of our research, attempting in this way to illuminate some of the problems faced by those charged with the task of making educational policy. (p. 285)

Levin (2004) also expressed a positive outlook on the role of research in developing education policy:

> Research is only one part of the way our societies make decisions about policy and practice. Other social and political forces will usually be more important and researchers will often feel that their work is ignored or misused. Nonetheless, growing interest in research and its potential contribution to policy and practice in education are heartening developments. While risks exist, and the results are unlikely ever to be as good as researchers might wish, there are steps that could be taken by all parties with an interest in education to strengthen the contribution of research to policy and practice in education. (pp. 16–17)

Although the relationship between research and policy is in no way clear or unambiguous, we must acknowledge that the *potential* for research significantly affecting education policy is considerable. Teachers may be somewhat doubtful about educational research, but their greater participation in policy research may allay some of those doubts.

One area of research not all that well known but that holds considerable potential is action research. In action research, teachers function as researchers and collaborate with others in the academic community to solve real-life problems and challenges at the classroom level. It is incumbent on the academic community, especially those in faculties of education, to enter into partnerships with teachers to explore action research opportunities. Such initiatives may help bolster the reputation of educational research and may improve future policy development and implementation.

Concluding Comment

This chapter has examined the relationship between research and policy. Depending on the perspective of the specific researcher, that relationship may be positive or negative, but it demands our attention. There exists a tremendous potential for educational research to have a significant effect on education policy in the future.

Chapter 11 discusses various issues and concerns inherent in the policy-making process.

DISCUSSION/REFLECTION QUESTIONS

1. Do you feel research has a role to play in the development of education policy? If so, what is that role?

2. What is your sense of the utility, or lack of utility, of educational research?

3. From your own experience as an educator, has research been used in policy development? If not, why?

4. Are educators receptive to being involved in research to develop effective education policies? Elaborate.

5. If educators are not receptive to being involved in research for policy development purposes, what steps might be taken and by whom to encourage educators to become more involved?

11

Issues and Concerns in Policy Development

Earlier chapters of this book concentrated on the practicalities of education policy. These practicalities have been gleaned from a variety of authors who have specialized in not only education policy but policy in general. This chapter examines several issues and concerns that have surfaced in the policy literature. Some of these issues and concerns also arise from my personal experience as a teacher and high school principal.

In no particular order of priority, the issues and concerns include stakeholder involvement in the policy-making process, the predominant model in the policy-making process, the politics and ethics of policy-making, equity in education policy, the link between policy and practice, and the effect media has on policy.

Stakeholder Involvement in the Policy-Making Process

According to Clemmer (1991), "board, administration, staff, parents, students, and the community as a whole profit from the greater understanding and improved communication that an effective policy development process engenders" (p. 33). This comment assumes there has been sufficient involvement by the various stakeholder groups in the process; such is not always the case. When people are insufficiently involved, much disenchantment occurs and morale suffers.

There have been attempts in many jurisdictions to strengthen the role of local voices—particularly those of parents—in the education system. These initiatives have seen the inclusion of different stakeholders and have sought to include a greater advisory or consultative role for parents in a broad range of school-related issues (Levin & Young, 1998). This has been done by giving legal status to a variety of parent advisory committees, school councils, and orientation committees at the school level, together with an elected membership and an expanded role in influencing the ongoing life of the school (Rideout, 1995). One of the more obvious roles for parent involvement is their input into the development of policies both at the building and district levels. In my experience, school boards have been relying on this kind of input increasingly over the last few years, and now it is quite common for school councils to be consulted on any new district initiative or policy. It is routine, of course, for the council to be involved in discussions related to initiatives and policies at the building level.

Concerns regarding the involvement of school councils center around the amount of input parents actually have and the degree to which their input is considered at the district level. Special interest groups are always a concern and there are indeed times when one has to wonder whether or not parents are able to see the big education picture. Ideally, feedback from parents through the school councils regarding district-wide issues should reflect those big-picture concerns; that is not always the case, however.

What role do teachers play in education policy? Sergiovanni et al. (1999) commented that

> nowhere has the power structure of education changed more rapidly with respect to the role teachers play in the development of policy. For well over a century, teachers in this country [United States] have been organizing to further the cause of education and, in the process, to advance their own interests in the realm of school politics. In the last four decades, the movement has gathered steam rapidly. Some would argue that their organizations are destined to become the dominant force in education policy, if they are not already. (p. 240)

Wirt and Kirst (1992) communicated a similar sentiment:

> No group has increased its influence on policy in recent decades as much as teachers. The timid rabbits of thirty years ago are today's ravaging tigers in the jungle of school systems. Unionism has produced this change, of course, and consequently made teachers a major political actor. (p. 207)

On a macro level, I have no argument with the previous statements. However, on a micro level—that is, at the district level—there appears to be concern that teachers are not as involved as they should be. Some also perceive that when teachers are involved in policy-making, they have limited influence or effect on the policy developed. I must acknowledge from my personal experience that teachers do have a significant influence on policies at the school level. This claim might seem obvious given that teachers are on the front lines of education each day and in constant contact with the school administrators. But the same is not necessarily the case when we discuss policy development at the district level.

Another group that has traditionally not been involved in the development of education policies is students. In several jurisdictions where school councils have been set up, legislation calls for a student to sit on the council; this legislation usually applies to high schools only. Levin and Young (1998) had this to say regarding student involvement in the policy-making process:

> Since students are commonly cited by all parties as the prime beneficiaries of schools, and the reason we have schools, it seems odd that they have typically had no formal role in making decisions about various aspects of schooling . . . . Considered from a political point of view, however, students have very little power. They lack organization, knowledge, wealth, and connections. As a result and despite the rhetoric, they can be—and often are—ignored when important decisions about their futures are being made. Where student involvement does exist, it is typically of a token nature, with little or no real influence on subsequent decisions. (p. 71)

Still, the trend appears to be toward broadening the composition of stakeholders involved in the education policy-making process. For instance, school councils may require a community member as part of their makeup. Various lobby groups may be consulted for their input as well. Gone are the days when policies were discussed and developed within the four walls of the schoolhouse or school district office. A major factor in this development is the role electronic media has played in reporting on the various education issues. Such reporting has heightened the awareness of parents and the community at large.

The Predominant Model in the Policy-Making Process

Although school-based management is currently undergoing a revival in education circles, I would suggest that the policy-making process has been primarily a top-down affair whereby those in power (e.g., the superintendent, the board) perceive a need for policy and act to serve that need. Theoretically, there should be widespread involvement at the grass-roots level. But we know historically that this is not always the case. Because of the highly politicized nature of the policy-making process, certain groups dominate the process. Levin and Young (1998) observed that

> in the case of education, the policy process is often dominated by the established groups—governments and stakeholder organizations. They are already organized, and tend to have staff and money. The people know and are used to dealing with one another. They are already present in many of the decision-making forums. This fact tends to push the policy process in particular directions. Each group normally acts to protect the welfare of its own members. If the key decisions are being made by people who are already part of the system and benefiting from it, there might well be less likelihood of significant change. Those most in need of the political process to advance their interests—children, poor people, recent immigrants— are often least able to mobilize themselves to take advantage of it. Aboriginal people have often been excluded from political participation. So were women: being denied the vote, being unable to own property in their own name, and being economically dependent on men made it very difficult for women to establish a vice in educational governance. (p. 73)

Although conceding that decision-making in education continues to be hierarchical, Owens (1998) did acknowledge a greater move toward collaboration:

> In traditional organizations [schools and school boards are prime examples], which are markedly hierarchical, the process of deciding how to make decisions is largely controlled by the administrator, not the followers. In such a case, the progress of the organization from autocratic decision making toward collaborative decision making resides largely in the extent to which the administrator sees power-sharing as a win-win proposition, a desirable state of affairs, rather than a threat to administrative hegemony. Many present-day educational organizations, though still hierarchical, have developed collaborative cultures to such an extent that reverting to the more primitive autocratic model would be difficult: the administrator is not so much confronted with the issue of whether or not others will be involved in the decision making but, rather, how and to what extent they will be involved. (p. 272)

It appears there is a movement to encourage greater involvement on the part of stakeholders. Perhaps this movement is due in part to much recent talk about organizations demonstrating greater transparency with respect to their internal machinations.

Rational vs. incremental

The policy-making process involves decision-making. According to Hill (1997), "the controversy about the way policies should be made has been a dispute between an approach which is distinctly prescriptive—rational decision-making theory—and alternatives of a more pragmatic kind, which suggest that decision making is 'incrementalist,' and that this offers the most effective way to reach accommodations between interests" (p. 99). The rational approach suggests that policy-making is done in a logical, comprehensive, and purposive manner (Simon, 1957).

Today, we are aware of so many more complexities in the policy-making process that we are no longer sure of the right way or the wrong way; even to think of policy-making in such terms would be an over-simplification. Lindblom (1959) has argued that policy-making seldom proceeds in a very rational manner; he painted a picture of an organization that, instead of finding optimal solutions to problems, staggered uncertainly toward marginally better ways of handling them. Braybrooke and Lindblom (1970) referred to this as the method of "successive approximations" (pp. 123–124)—that is, incrementalism.

Sergiovanni et al. (1999) summarized incrementalism as perceived by Lindblom and his followers:

> Gone was the notion of wise men sitting around solving recurring problems for all time. Replacing it was a notion of fallible human beings, limited in their abilities to see very far ahead, unable to examine all conceivable alternatives, settling for the first suggestion that promised to yield better results than the present policy. Lindblom and others who saw the same kind of limitations on rational policy making became known as *incrementalists*, and Lindblom (1959) dubbed his view the process of "muddling through." (p. 231)

From a practitioner's perspective, we might agree that policy-making does not happen in a rational manner. Rather, as Lindblom and others have suggested, I believe that "muddling through" is an appropriate description of a process in education that in recent years has attempted to involve stakeholders at the grass roots. It is reasonable to conclude, however, that while there have been legitimate attempts to make that involvement happen, the challenge of actually having stakeholders meaningfully involved in the process still remains.

The Politics and Ethics of Policy-Making

We might like to think that all decisions and policies in education are

developed and undertaken with the best interests of students as the ultimate objective. However, the reality is that this is not always so. Fullan
(1991) referred to educational change as a "snarled process" (p. 50).
Because education policy is all about change, the phrase *snarled process*
could also be used to describe policy-making.

Thompson (1976) has defined politics as "the struggle over the allocation of social values and resources" that "involves making choices" (p. 3).
Quoting Lasswell's definition of "who gets what, when and where,"
Thompson (1976) further suggested that "politics connotes the idea of
people using influence and power to effect policies agreeable with their
preferences" (p. 3). Both at the building and district levels, politics per-
meates the decision-making process. The importance of values in policy-
making was discussed in chapter 2. The political process is the medium by
which those values are allocated. Education policy-making is absolutely
about values; it is also about the allocation of resources, both financial and
human, of which there are never enough to go around.

Politics involves individuals who come together for the purposes of
solidarity and strength. In many jurisdictions in Canada and the United
States, for example, education reform has involved reorganization of school
systems and the resultant closure of school buildings with a whole list of
related issues; these actions have encouraged people to band together in
efforts to force education bureaucracies, whether they be school boards or
ministries of education, to reverse various decisions. Policy is developed in
an environment where politics is rampant; policy-makers must necessarily
be prepared to be responsive.

Enter the ethical perspectives on policy-making. Ethics is about doing
the right thing for the right reasons. We might conclude that ethics is
fairly straightforward, but the waters become surprisingly muddied when
politics is thrown in as another ingredient in the policy-making process.
Balance is the operative word. The onus is on those involved in policy-
making to achieve balance by keeping in mind and considering the various political pressures and ethical concerns—particularly the needs and
wants of communities that may be locally under-represented.

I am not convinced that this balance is always achieved; whether ethical concerns are consistently taken into consideration is debatable at the
best of times. The solution to this concern is not an easy one. Suffice to
say that from my point of view, those overseeing the policy process must
ensure that balance is found.

Equity in Education Policy

Equity is often defined in terms of equality of educational opportunity (Imber, 2001, p. 33). The concern here is whether or not education policy addresses this notion of educational opportunity. Imber (2001) emphasized the point that

> every education policy maker and practitioner—from legislator and school board member to administrator and classroom teacher—is involved in the allocation of educational resources. While we often conceive of educational resources in terms of money (per-pupil expenditures), in reality they consist of a varied set of goods and services, and teacher time, attention, and expertise. Together these goods and services make up the value of the education a student receives. (p. 33)

From Imber's (2001) viewpoint, education policy and practice must be designed to promote the goal of creating the most equitable system of education possible. He explained his perspective on equity in policy-making:

> Equity should not be understood in terms of inputs, such as whether an equal amount of money is spent on each pupil, because the same input can benefit some pupils much more than others. Nor should equity be understood in terms of outputs because achieving the same outputs with all pupils is neither possible nor socially desirable. Rather, equity must be understood in terms of opportunity. All students have the right to benefit commensurate with the opportunity provided to other students. (p. 34)

Another way of looking at equity is in terms of fairness. A basic question that all policy-makers need to ask themselves is whether the policy being contemplated is fair to those who will be most affected by it. Several authors (e.g., Taylor et al., 1997) discussed equity in terms of social justice; this may be a more appropriate conceptualization.

A classic argument might have to do with a school district's per-pupil grant to schools; a similar argument can be made when discussing provincial/state grants to school districts. Should the grant to schools in an affluent part of the district be the same as that to schools in an economically depressed area where unemployment is rampant and achievement levels are considerably below what they should be? In terms of fairness or social justice, one would probably respond that they should not be. Equality and equity are often used interchangeably; however, in the question just posed, an equal dollar amount does not mean equity has been achieved. Nowhere is the value-laden nature of policy-making more obvious than when discussing the provision of resources to educational organizations.

I suggest we take the concept of equity into consideration when education policies are being developed and implemented. We must acknowledge the complexity of the policy-making process: aspects of that process, including development and implementation, are never black and white. In the current climate of declining resources, both financial and human, those charged with developing policies have difficult decisions to make. It is our best hope that the notion of equity in education be given the attention it rightfully deserves.

The Link Between Policy and Practice

Classroom teachers are the recipients of many of the dicta resulting from education policies. It is common to hear teachers comment that they are not interested in policy development as it is something that should be left to "administrative types" such as principals and school board officials. The major concern of teachers is the relevance of policy to what they actually do in the classroom: teach. One reason for this perspective is that education policy has traditionally been preoccupied with issues of governance and administration; pedagogy is very seldom addressed in education policy.

Clune (1993) spoke to this concern:

> Educational policy is typically fragmented and ineffective, producing a great volume of uncoordinated mandates, programs, and projects that provide no coherent direction, increase the complexity of educational governance and practice, and consume a lot of resources. The United States produces the largest quantity of educational policy in the world, and the least effective. (pp. 126–127)

Bosetti (1991) called for a more practical approach:

> more could be accomplished by the growing efforts to find the "correct" policy solution in real life contexts. Academics can all too easily fall into the trap of trying to develop theory to explain reality, albeit imperfectly and then conduct critical analyses from the perspective that they should match theory. (p. 219)

Policies are the very foundation of schooling. Whether it be in the school or at the district level, it is in the best interest of teachers to pay more attention to policy. Policy ultimately dictates what happens at the building and in the classroom, where teachers do their daily work.

Caldwell and Spinks (1988) acknowledged the difficulties associated with linking policies to programs:

> Policies are statements about substantive issues, including the curriculum, that contain the purposes to be achieved and the broad

guidelines by which they can be achieved. Policy statements are prepared about such issues as mathematics, assessment of students, discipline, and reporting to parents. Programmes are natural divisions of the curriculum that reflect how the school is organised and how teachers work and children learn. Just as the set of policies will differ from school to school, so will the set of programmes. Some policies will link directly to programmes; for example, the policies on mathematics and physical education will be reflected in Mathematics and Physical Education Programmes, respectively, in most schools. However, this will not always be the case with all curriculum-related policies in all schools. (p. 115)

If we think about it at all, it is obvious how important policies are to institutions such as schools. But we need to keep in mind that policy-making in various institutions and organizations is affected by outside influences. Our discussion now turns to one of those influences.

The Effect of Media on Policy

When I use the term *media*, I am not only referring to television, radio, newspapers, and magazines (print media). Emerging at an unprecedented rate, social media is influencing all aspects of life in the twenty-first century, and its impact on policy development is no exception.

According to Marshall and Gerstl-Pepin (2005), "the media is a discursive arena that serves as the primary avenue through which most citizens receive information about policy issues and thus can support participatory democracy and encourage citizenship" (p. 123). They went on to state, somewhat critically, that

> often media do not: Only certain perspectives are deemed legitimate for coverage, and due to space limitations, not all perspectives are always presented. Critically examining media coverage (or a lack of coverage) of policy issues offers insights into policy-maker strategies and possible public or special interest group resistance. Noting which issues are ignored or are framed in limited ways can also provide a way of exploring which issues are ignored or "silenced." (p. 123)

Facebook, Twitter, and many thousands of opinion-leading bloggers rapidly transmit ideas about schooling and policy that are framed in sometimes overtly biased ways. Their amplification can be good or bad.

Wu, Ramesh, Howlett, and Fritzen (2010) also acknowledged the significant role of media in policy-making:

> In societies with a relatively free press, the media can also play an important role in bringing issues onto the public and government agendas. The development of information and communication

technologies has greatly empowered the media to share public opinion on public problems. Their ability to name and blame a policy for
a problem can sometimes force an issue onto the agenda. (p. 15)

However, there is a school of thought out there that suggests government overplays the role of media in its development of policy. Fairclough
(2000) commented that "a media strategy is prepared for all significant
government initiatives—they are 'trailed' in the media before being
properly launched, and there is a systematic 'follow-up.' This has been
described as 'government by media spin'" (p. 122). Remember, though,
that Fairclough made this observation before the emergence of social
media platforms. Perhaps today's "sharing" culture is simply a new, faster
way for the government, and other agencies, to get their messages out.

In the ideal world, we would see education policy development,
informed by research, emanating from the field or the school system,
reflecting the needs of key stakeholders—students, teachers, administrators, and parents—who are most affected by education policy. However,
I am concerned that we commonly see governments and school boards
develop policies from a macro perspective and then float "trial balloons"
to ascertain how the public might react to such policies. Participation at
the stakeholder level is often ignored, and policies are developed, formalized, and then thrust upon those very stakeholders who were ignored in
the process. Media is sometimes a naive partner with government as radio
and television talk shows, online surveys, and various social media provide
fodder for government to initiate policy development.

Concluding Comment

This chapter has articulated several issues related to education policy.
Perhaps the greatest challenge for today's education practitioner is to
see the utility of the policy in everyday practice. The time devoted to
policy development at the school level is woefully inadequate and this
may account for the disdain teachers often exhibit toward policy. How to
bridge that perceptual gap is a challenge to which there is no easy answer.

Chapter 12 considers the role of policy in education reform.

DISCUSSION/REFLECTION QUESTIONS

1. Several concerns have been identified in chapter 11. List at least two
   other concerns related to education policy that you have personally
   experienced in your everyday practice. Attempt to articulate
   solutions to these concerns.

2. In your experience, is the top-down model of policy development and implementation changing to a more grass-roots model? Elaborate.

3. At the building level, are issues and concerns regarding education policy—whether it be policy developed in the building itself, at the school district level, or at the ministry of education—articulated regularly? If not, why? If so, what form does that articulation take? Does it result in positive action?

4. How do you see the role of media, including social media, affecting the process of policy-making?

12

Policy and Education Reform

Education Reform

Education reform seems to have been, and perhaps continues to be, the key term in education in recent years. *Education reform* is often discussed in terms of *educational change*; indeed, from many perspectives the terms could be interchangeable. This chapter examines the role policy plays in the reform process.

Taylor et al. (1997) described the relationship between policy and reform:

> References to change have now become ubiquitous in politics and policy. At the same time few, if any, policies are entirely new: most are shaped by characteristics of previous policies . . . . Policy is thus an instrument through which change is mapped onto existing policies, programmes or organisations, and onto the demands made by particular interest groups. To put forward a policy is to acknowl-edge that a new policy was needed or that the old policy needed to be revised in response to the changes occurring in society. (p. 5)

Any educational change process brings with it a myriad of challenges for those in the trenches. McLaughlin (1998) commented on those chal-lenges:

> teachers confront unprecedented demands for reform—calls for teachers to do better, and to do differently than they have done before. Efforts to raise standards for what students are expected to learn take place in the context of a "revolution" in cognitive science. New theories of learning frame new conceptions about impor-tant outcomes of learning and, by extension, ideas about school:

higher-order thinking skills and deep understanding of the conceptual structures of knowledge domains take center stage in classroom
instruction. Implied is a classroom environment more responsive to
diverse student abilities and interests, where instruction emphasizes
cooperative learning strategies, provides direct opportunities to construct knowledge and understanding, and incorporates performance
assessments that tap students' conceptual development rather than
mastery of rote knowledge. The extent to which teachers can succeed in meeting these goals depends on their success in wrestling
with the deep, hard changes in beliefs, attitudes, and practices they
assume. (p. 82)

Such expectations represent megachallenges for today's teachers. We
now recognize that students come through our school doors carrying a
multitude of issues with them: poverty and unemployment, physical and
sexual abuse, inadequate parenting, family illness, single-parent families,
lack of nutrition, lack of sleep, and cyberbullying, just to mention a few.
This kind of baggage exacerbates the challenges teachers face every day.
We can merely ponder whether reforms such as those listed are realistic
and achievable.

Reforms necessitate major changes in individual school operations and
organization. Cohen and Spillane (1993) were less than optimistic as to
the attainability of such changes:

One reason is that teachers and administrators would have a great
deal to learn. It is unlikely they could offer the intellectually ambitious instruction that reformers seek unless they had ample time to
learn on the job. Another reason is that the new instruction would
be much more complex and demanding than the common fare in
schools today. It is unlikely that teachers could do such work unless
they had the autonomy to make complicated decisions, to work with
colleagues, and to revise as they went. Still another reason is that
teachers could hardly contribute to the development of a common
instructional system unless they had much more time and opportunities to work with others in education beyond their school. How
could these changes be made in the context of reforms that entail
much greater central authority and power? This could not be done
easily, unless the reforms were carefully designed to enhance such
autonomy, and unless the capacities to exercise it were nurtured at all
levels of education. (p. 81)

Similarly, O'Day and Smith (1993) pointed out that the need for
instructional reform is taken for granted in most policy circles (p. 263).
They comment further that

as official bodies endorse it [instructional reform] at national and state levels, as organizations of experts design national and state content frameworks and standards, and as curriculum and test developers redesign their materials to meet the new criteria, the concept of challenging content and higher-order skills takes on an aura of official policy. And with that aura of policy comes the responsibility of governments. Simple justice dictates that skills and knowledge deemed *necessary* for basic citizenship and economic opportunity be available to *all* future citizens—that is, access must be distributed equally, not just equitably. (p. 263)

We may get the impression that the call for educational reform has legitimated the forging of new policies. An obvious inherent danger is that the development of such policies can occur fairly quickly, but the actual implementation, with the requisite in-service work with stakeholders, occurs at a much slower (some might say glacial) pace. Taylor et al. (1997) have suggested that

the term "reform" has become one of the most over-used ideas in the political vocabulary. It presupposes legitimacy and invites support for the ideas propagated in the particular policy. In this way, therefore, the state is not neutral with respect to the changes occurring in society, and its own interest in sponsoring some changes and preventing others is reflected in policy. (p. 5)

Darling-Hammond (1998) made the point that "policymakers who want teachers to succeed at new kinds of teaching must understand that the process of change requires time and opportunities for teachers to reconstruct their practice through intensive study and experimentation" (p. 654). She listed four obligations of policies necessary to achieve this:

1. Policies should first create extensive *learning opportunities* for teachers, administrators, parents, and community members so that complex practices envisioned by ambitious learning goals have a chance to be studied, debated, tried out, analyzed, retried, and refined until they are well understood and incorporated into the repertoire of those who teach and make decisions in schools.
2. Policies should allow for widespread *engagement* of a school's constituencies in the process of considering, developing, and enacting changes. For this to occur, communities must have a substantial role in constructing their own reforms rather than trying merely to implement ideas handed down to them

by others—ideas that are bound to be poorly understood and mistrusted unless there is an opportunity to create adaptations that are valued and appropriate in the local context.

3. Policies should recognize the need for *simultaneous change* in all regularities of schooling that influence the possibilities for successful teaching of this kind. This means rethinking the array of policies—from school funding to teacher education to school accreditation to collective bargaining rules—that hold the current regularities of schooling so firmly in place.

4. Policies should be constructed in ways that maintain the *delicate balance* between external standards that press for improvement and the school autonomy needed to create an engine for internal change. (pp. 654–655)

For the past several decades, education practitioners—teachers and school administrators—have been inundated with calls for education reform. Policies have attempted to facilitate such reform. In fact, one could say—somewhat facetiously, perhaps even sarcastically—that industries have been spawned by the proliferation of literature on a multitude of bandwagon fads in education. Perhaps the only ones who have really benefitted from this proliferation are the companies and the academics who develop and sell this literature. Practitioners are overwhelmed by all this activity, and very often their response is to think something like "Why can't the powers that be back off and give us the time to do what we are supposed to do in this profession: teach!" This may be a rather cynical view of reform, but I also think it is a realistic one.

Concluding Comment

Education reform and related education policies have not always been perceived as relevant to front-line practitioners. Yet the current literature seems to suggest that front-line educators' involvement is a *sine qua non*: without such involvement, reforms aimed at improving current classroom practice are doomed to fail. Education policies have a significant role to play in the reform movement. They are the vehicle by which reforms can be initiated and legitimated. But practitioners must be intimately involved in development and implementation.

Chapter 13 details a specific study examining various challenges and concerns in developing and implementing education policy.

DISCUSSION/REFLECTION QUESTIONS

1. What does the term *education reform* mean to you?

2. What kinds of education reforms have you personally experienced as an educator?

3. What do you perceive to be the relationship, if any, between policy and education reform?

4. Is education reform a finite concept meaning that it happens and then it is done? Elaborate.

5. How is education reform perceived by education practitioners in general?

13

A Research Study on Education Policy

This chapter outlines a research study I undertook, titled *Challenges and Concerns in Developing and Implementing Education Policy* (Delaney, 2007). The study looked at various aspects of the education policy process.

Purpose of the Study

This was a regional study that involved interviewing various stakeholders in education (students, teachers, school and district administrators, and parents) about what they perceive as challenges and concerns in developing and implementing education policy.

Perspectives

The literature on developing and implementing education policy deals with these challenges and concerns (i.e., problems) from a macro perspective (Caldwell & Spinks, 1988; Bosetti, 1991; Clune, 1993; Owens, 1998; Fairclough, 2000; Imber, 2001). Very little attention has been paid in the literature to the micro perspectives regarding various problems experienced by the major stakeholders in education. By *micro perspectives* I mean practical, down-to-earth problems practitioners experience daily.

Mode of Inquiry

The mode of inquiry used in this study is qualitative: one-on-one interviews consisting of eight in-depth questions. Each interview took approximately 45 to 60 minutes to complete. Interviews were conducted with 30 study participants: students, teachers, parents, and school and district administrators.

Results

My findings have been organized under three headings: participant perspectives, emergent themes, and suggested solutions/strategies.

Participant perspectives
Student

1. Students' opinions regarding education policy are not often solicited. When they are, they are not always valued and respected.
2. School policies are often "passed down" to students without rationales or explanations.
3. Today's policies don't always address concerns and challenges in today's classrooms.
4. The "busyness" of teachers and school administrators very often prevents their taking the time to talk to students about school, district, and provincial policies that affect them.

Parent

1. District offices don't always acknowledge the value of input from school (advisory) councils.
2. High school students lack knowledge about the policy-making process and the policies that affect them on a daily basis.
3. School districts don't always take into consideration how district policies will affect individual schools and their communities.
4. Students perceive that their input is not valued and hence, not wanted.

School (Teachers and School Administrators)

1. There is a significant lack of parental involvement and input into the policy-making process.
2. School legislation is out of date and in serious need of updating.
3. There is an overabundance of paperwork associated with various policies.
4. With the recently created "supersized" school districts in this geographical area, there is a heightened lack of awareness of the tremendous differences among the regions.

District

1. District physical geographies often impede bringing together various stakeholders.

2. Policy-making is slow.
3. There is a lack of substitute time to facilitate teachers serving on school and district-wide committees involved in developing policies.
4. District and provincial policy-making can detract from the local autonomy of schools; consequently, schools perceive themselves as "victims of policy" as opposed to being active participants in the policy-making process.

Emergent themes

1. a move toward greater centralization of decision-making at the departmental/ministry level
2. the supersizing of school districts having a negative impact on the school–district relationship
3. the under-resourcing (human and financial) of school districts by the provincial government having a negative effect on the credibility of school districts
4. time (or a lack thereof) being a major issue for stakeholders with respect to policy-making
5. a sincere interest on the part of stakeholders to be meaningfully involved in policy-making
6. a genuine desire on the part of stakeholders to develop policies designed to improve their schools

Suggested solutions/strategies

1. When developing policy, it is important to keep in mind that flexibility (i.e., "wiggle room") is necessary to accommodate the multitude of stakeholders' perspectives on various school-related issues.
2. Schools and district offices should encourage and promote wide involvement of stakeholders and take the time necessary to garner meaningful input.
3. District offices should assign a senior management position dedicated solely to overseeing and directing the policy-making process.
4. High schools should develop and formalize a process whereby senior students (Grades 10–12) be given the opportunity

to become meaningfully engaged in policy-making (e.g., opinionnaires, focus groups, student discussion forums).

5. Schools and district offices should establish formal communication links (e.g., digital communication) to facilitate a greater understanding of and appreciation for the importance of policy-making.

6. District offices should formalize the active involvement and participation of school councils in policy-making.

7. The Ministry of Education should provide release time for teachers to be involved in school, district, and provincial committee work related to policy-making.

8. There should be a greater sharing of information related to policy-making between school districts (e.g., by developing a template for information sharing).

9. Schools, school districts, and the Ministry of Education should use the expertise in policy-making at the local university and various other agencies in the university.

Concluding Comment

There is a considerable amount of literature dedicated to the big-picture or macro issues in developing and implementing education policy. However, there is a dearth of literature concentrating on the micro issues surrounding education policy. This study provides considerable insight into those issues from the perspectives of various stakeholders in education. The study brings forth several solutions and strategies for reflection and consideration.

Chapter 14 discusses the future of education policy.

DISCUSSION/REFLECTION QUESTIONS

1. Should research on education policy be conducted from a micro or a macro perspective, or from both? Justify your choice.

2. Who should conduct research on education policy? Why?

3. What aspects of education policy should be researched? Why?

4. What do you perceive to be the greatest challenge in conducting research on education policy? Why?

14

The Future of Education Policy

What lies in the future for education policy? Will it gain greater prominence than it has had in the past, or will it continue to be relegated to the back burners? These questions are not easily answered but do deserve some reflection.

In chapter 1, I stated that our recent preoccupation with education policy was characterized by Silver (1995) as "policy rage" (p. 2). I contend that policy rage shows no sign of relenting; indeed, I might suggest that it will be amplified in the next few years. Why might this be so? Given the current pace of reform in education, coupled with an ever-increasing emphasis on (perhaps even paranoia over) liability concerns, policy will necessarily take on even greater prominence in school and school district governance.

Over the past several decades, we have looked to education to cure our social, economic, and political problems. Schools have responded by taking on new, noneducational roles: those of the surrogate parent, the social worker, the police officer, and the pharmacist, to mention a few. Policies have been developed in an attempt to clarify these new roles for educators. What had resulted previously were policy manuals large enough to act as doorstoppers and that were rarely consulted because of their sheer size and their legalese. Today, the large binders that housed these manuals are gone and policies live on institutional web pages, readily available at the click of a mouse.

Coombs (1994) has suggested that if our social context continues to change so rapidly, "it is doubtful that much that we think we know about how education policy is formulated will be true 20 years from now" (p. 607). He elaborates:

> Tensions between the profession and the lay public will change in
> character as both the profession and the orientations of the public
> change. Relationships between the various levels of educational
> policy making may change dramatically. It is difficult to identify
> laws, propositions, or even common knowledge that we confidently
> believe will survive these changes. (p. 607)

It seems to me that there is a basic cynicism out there with respect to all kinds of policy; this cynicism might be more prevalent in the field of education. I have shared some of my own cynicism with you in the previous chapter. In education specifically, I think we need to step back and assess where policy has gotten us over the past several years. There have been policy plusses and policy minuses. And so, in this chapter, we consider the need for more basic research, which might improve the quality of our policies in education.

More Basic Research

Coombs (1994) identified the need for more basic research on education policy as a priority in the years ahead:

> Impatience with the limited payoff of basic research in education to
> date has prompted some to suggest that research efforts should be
> redirected toward applied research that would yield immediate divi-
> dends in the improvement of schools. There is, however, no certain
> way to improve educational outcomes without improving our knowl-
> edge of the policy process. (p. 607)

Coombs (1994) named policy relevance as a major concern of the research that has been conducted. He recommended that more research was needed probing the linkages between the preferences of constituents and the policy process as well as research examining the connection between education policy and changes in educational outcomes (p. 607). He continued:

> For basic research to be policy relevant, it is necessary to identify
> variables that are alterable through policy change and that will also
> bring about the kind of educational outcomes we seek. Until we have
> a much better idea of how interventions are likely to affect a student's
> academic achievement, conduct, attitudes (including educational
> aspirations), or access to continued schooling, for example, policy
> analysis is likely to continue to be a sometimes futile exercise. (p. 607)

Finally, Coombs (1994) made these suggestions with respect to the use of policy specialists outside the education arena:

Attention to the demographic, social or economic changes that precipitate changes in education policy will require expertise from specialists in those areas. Closer examination of the impact of education policy on students will require methodological sophistication and intuition about schooling more likely to be found among educational researchers. Knowledge of the policy process alone leaves us far short of the capability to foresee changes in the environment that will stimulate new policy proposals, to predict the educational outcomes of proposed alternatives with confidence, and to make timely adjustments. Education policy analysis will have come of age when its theories and its methods are equal to that task. (p. 608)

Policy Coherence

Coupled with the call for greater policy relevance with respect to educational research is a concern with the lack of policy coherence. Cibulka (1999) noted that

the American system of public education is characterized by a lack of coherent policies extending from the federal level down to the local school, and extending laterally to other institutions such as employers. At the state level, for example, there seldom are policies that attempt to align policies pertaining to curriculum, student assessment, teacher certification, and professional development, and finance. What is needed, in other words, is "systemic reform" so that policies and practices are more tightly coupled. (p. 176)

Similarly, Fuhrman (1993) wrote

a crisis of confidence surrounds education policy. Reformers despair of the failure of the "top-down reforms" of the early 1980s and of the unfulfilled promise of the "bottom-up," school-by-school change efforts of the later 1980s. The ability of the political system to deliver quality schooling is under attack. Many argue that policies should be abandoned altogether—by completely substituting market control or by removing policies so that schools can improve themselves unfettered. (p. 28)

All is not lost, however. Fuhrman (1993) offered another approach for our consideration:

However, the abandonment of policy does not offer hope of widespread improvement because schools cannot sustain self-generated change. Nor is school-by-school change likely to spread to all schools. The system must offer support. Systemic reform approaches suggest a way that the system can support school change, without

either stifling school initiative or leaving schools to fare for themselves without help from the wider policy environment. Systemic
reform approaches offer another possibility for those disappointed
by policy, an approach to policy that combines centralized leadership
around outcomes with decentralized decision making about practice.
(p. 28)

There are obviously legitimate concerns regarding policy development
in general. As I noted earlier, these concerns seem to be more acute in
the field of education, perhaps because of the unique nature of the education organization and the education system. There are no easy answers to
the education policy issues I discuss throughout this book. One partial
answer, however, might be that stakeholders need to be more involved in
the policy-making process; in practice, however, being involved is easier
said than done. Such involvement may be facilitated by organizations
such as school boards taking more time in "educating" those stakeholders
as to the intricacies of education policy and why education policy-making
should exist to improve the lot of our students.

Systemic Education Policy

Congruent with Fuhrman's thinking, Clune (1993) put forth the concept of *systemic education policy*, the idea behind which is "that the current
policy goal of substantial increases in student achievement will require
a major shift in a large number of educational policies" (p. 125). Clune
(1993) suggests the following five characteristics of systemic policy are
worth considering:

1. research-based goals for changes in educational practice and
   organization;
2. working models of new practice and professionally accessible
   knowledge;
3. a centralized/decentralized change process;
4. regular assessment of educational inputs, outcomes, and process;
5. a coherent, sustained, change-oriented political process.
   (pp. 127–130)

Although I would argue that systemic education policy is being developed to some degree at the present, those efforts are at best piecemeal.
Much more needs to be done to bring about the results we desire. School
improvement is the big-picture goal of systemic education policy, so significant increases in student achievement represent a major part of that

goal. If education policy is to regain the stature and respect it warrants (if it ever had it in the first place), significant gains must be made by the key players in the education policy arena.

Concluding Comment

In the introduction to this chapter, a couple of questions were posed: *What lies ahead for education policy? Will education policy take on a greater prominence than it has in the past or will it be relegated to the back burners?* My comments here have attempted to address those queries. Unless educators attach relevance and coherence to the policy-making process and the policies that result, education policy may go the way of the dodo bird.

DISCUSSION/REFLECTION QUESTIONS

1. In your opinion, is there a future for education policy? Elaborate.

2. In your opinion, what needs to happen for education policy to take on a greater importance in the lives of education practitioners?

3. Centralized versus decentralized decision-making: where does education policy-making fit? Elaborate.

4. Generally speaking, are educators concerned about the state of education policy? Why or why not?

5. What is one major concern that today's educators have with education policy? Elaborate.

15

Concluding Thoughts

This book has endeavored to provide a comprehensive and practical overview of various aspects of education policy. Those aspects include what is meant by education policy along with the many facets of the policymaking process: the values and principles inherent in education policy, types of education policy, policy analysis, policy development, policy implementation, policy evaluation, and policy dissemination. The book also discussed policy and regulations and offered a sampling of concerns currently being experienced in education policy, exemplified in the synopsis of a study presented in chapter 13. The role of policy in education reform and the future of education policy was also explored.

Although this approach to education policy has been somewhat linear, I fully realize that in the real world of education—students, teachers, parents, administrators, school board personnel, board trustees and the day-to-day complexities of teaching and learning—education policy is anything but linear. Linear evokes images of clarity and simplicity. Education policy, encompassing real-life intricacies and complexities, is not like that. The linear approach does suffice when one is writing a book like this or when one is giving a neat and tidy lecture on the topic. However, it is imperative that students of education policy recognize the complexity and messiness that is the reality of the policy worker.

To underline the significance of these complexities, I observe that the mechanics of education policy are important, but only to the degree that they allow the student to realize that education policy is indeed complex. Education policy reflects a "snarled process" (Fullan, 2001, p. 50), but in an arena that affects so much of our lives, throughout our lives, perhaps we should expect nothing less.

The Purpose of Education Policy

What is the purpose of education policy? Perhaps naively and a little unre-alistically, I have suggested here that education policy should exist for the improvement of teaching and learning. In fact, Fuhrman (1993) went so far as to state that "improving teaching and learning is at the heart of coherent education policy" (p. 320). Unfortunately, the educational waters get very muddied by such realities as the politics of education and a whole host of concomitant issues and concerns. And ultimately, as is so common and widespread in education, what is for the good of the student—the improvement of teaching and learning—tends to get lost in the big picture.

The Role of Teachers

McLaughlin (1987) has made the point that in education, it is the small-est unit, the classroom, that ultimately determines the effectiveness of education policy (p. 143). Classroom teachers are at the center of teach-ing and learning. It is therefore of paramount importance that teach-ers understand "how policy can enable and facilitate" their work in the classroom (McLaughlin, 1991, p. 155). How such understanding may be accomplished indeed remains the challenge for policy-makers. Accord-ing to Taylor et al. (1997), education policy does not deal directly with teaching and learning and "the implications of policies for these practices . . . are often left unstated and certainly under-theorized" (p. 173). Thus, teachers fail to see the value of many education policies.

If greater attention were paid to teachers' interests in the policy-making process, then presumably more teachers would be more involved with and pay more attention to education policy. For teachers, then, a proactive approach, as opposed to a reactive one, is an advantage. But the proactive approach is indeed a challenge teachers face in an era when practitioners are constantly expected to do more with less—less money, fewer human resources.

The Role of School-Level Administrators

Although many of the comments in the previous section may apply to the work of school administrators, there are also areas where education policies affect administrators directly. Granted, these have more to do with school governance issues and concerns; the challenge of connecting school governance with teaching and learning remains. This is a challenge administrators should be capable of meeting. Given the sheer volume of the literature on school reform, school improvement, and educational change, the resources do exist and are very accessible.

Again, I endorse a proactive approach on the part of administrators, while acknowledging that taking such an approach is obviously easier said than done. Given the multitude of demands on administrators' daily agendas, no simple answer to these challenges is forthcoming.

In Conclusion

Education policy should serve to guide and facilitate our work as educators, whether we are teachers in the classroom, building administrators, or school board officials. Education policy in the big picture should serve to guide and facilitate teaching and learning. Unfortunately, as suggested previously, we very often get mired down in the politics of education and as a result, students suffer.

Policy can be restrictive and regressive if we allow it to be so. On the other hand, policy can guide us and facilitate the important work of teaching and learning. Policy then becomes the medium by which we do that work—nothing more, nothing less.

DISCUSSION/REFLECTION QUESTIONS

1. Generally speaking, is education policy perceived by education practitioners to be something of value and utility, or is it more of that "theoretical stuff" taught in faculties of education that has no practicality and relevance to the day-to-day work of teaching and administering schools?

2. Is education policy alive and well in your jurisdiction? Elaborate.

3. Now that you have worked your way through this book, consider again how you would design a graduate course on education policy studies. Has your perspective changed?

References

Alexander, N. A. (2013). *Policy analysis for educational leaders*. Boston: Pearson.

Ball, S. J. (1994). *Education reform: A critical and post-structural approach*. Buckingham, UK: Open University.

Berliner, D. C. (1990). Research on teaching and educational policy. In L. R. Marcus & B. D. Stickney (Eds.), *Politics and policy in the age of education* (pp. 263–287). Springfield, IL: Charles C. Thomas.

Bosetti, R. (1991). The policy process in Alberta Education. In R. R. O'Reilly & C. J. Lautar (Eds.) *Policy research and development in Canadian education* (pp. 211–221). Calgary, AB: University of Calgary.

Boyd, W. (1988). Policy analysis, educational policy, and management: Through a glass darkly? In N. Boyan (Ed.), *Handbook of research on educational administration* (pp. 501–522). White Plains, NY: Longman.

Boyd, W. L., & Plank, D. N. (1994). *The international encyclopedia of education* (2nd ed.). New York: Pergamon.

Braybrooke, D., & Lindblom, C. E. (1970). *A strategy of decision: Policy evaluation as a social process*. New York: Free Press.

Brown, J. (1996). Policy and policymaking. In L. B. Sheppard & J. Brown (Eds.), *Educational administration: Theory and practice* (pp. 1–30). St. John's, NF: Memorial University of Newfoundland.

Caldwell, B. J., & Spinks, J. M. (1988). *The self-managing school*. Philadelphia, PA: Falmer.

Carley, M. (1980). *Rational techniques in policy analysis*. Aldershot, UK: Gower.

Cibulka, J. G. (1999). Ideological lenses for interpreting political and economic changes affecting schooling. In J. Murphy & K. Seashore Louis (Eds.), *Handbook of research on educational administration* (pp. 163–182). San Francisco: Jossey-Bass.

Clemmer, E. F. (1991). *The school policy handbook*. Needham Heights, MA: Allyn and Bacon.

Clune, W. H. (1993). Systemic educational policy: A conceptual framework. In S. H. Fuhrman (Ed.), *Designing coherent education policy: Improving the system* (pp. 125–140). San Francisco: Jossey-Bass.

Cohen, D. K., & Garet, M. S. (1991). Reforming education policy with applied social research. In D. S. Anderson & B. J. Biddle (Eds.), *Knowledge for policy: Improving education through research* (pp. 123–140). Bristol, PA: Falmer.

Cohen, D. K., & Spillane, J. P. (1993). Policy and practice: The relations between governance and instruction. In S. H. Fuhrman (Ed.), *Designing coherent education policy: Improving the system* (pp. 35–95). San Francisco: Jossey-Bass.

Colebatch, H. K. (1998). *Policy*. Minneapolis: University of Minnesota.

Coombs, F. S. (1994). Education policy. In S. S. Nagel (Ed.), *Encyclopedia of policy studies* (pp. 587–615). New York: Dekker.

Cunningham, C. (1963). Policy and practice. *Public Administration, 41*(3), 229–238. https://doi.org/10.1111/j.1467-9299.1963.tb01786.x

Darling-Hammond, L. (1998). Policy and change: Getting beyond bureaucracy. In A. Hargreaves, A. Lieberman, M. Fullan, & D. Hopkins (Eds.), *International handbook of educational change* (pp. 642–667). Dordrecht, The Netherlands: Kluwer.

Delaney, J. G. (2007). *Challenges and concerns in developing and implementing education policy. A doctoral seminar presentation to the Faculty of Education.* St. John's, NL: Memorial University of Newfoundland.

Downey, L. W. (1988). *Policy analysis in education*. Calgary, AB: Detselig.

Duke, D. L., & Canady, R. L. (1991). *School policy*. New York: McGraw-Hill.

Elmore, R., & McLaughlin, M. (1983). The federal role in education: Learning from experience. *Education and Urban Society, 15*(3), 309–330. https://doi.org/10.1177/0013124583015003004

Fairclough, N. (2000). *New labour, new language?* London: Routledge.

Finn, C. E. (1991). What ails education research? In D. S. Anderson & B. J. Biddle (Eds.), *Knowledge for policy: Improving education through research* (pp. 39–42). Bristol, PA: Falmer.

First, P. F. (1992). *Educational policy for school administrators*. Needham Heights, MA: Allyn and Bacon.

Fowler, F. C. (2009). *Policy studies for educational leaders: An introduction* (3rd ed.). Boston: Pearson.

Fuhrman, S. H. (1993). The politics of coherence. In S. H. Fuhrman (Ed.), *Designing coherent education policy: Improving the system* (pp. 1–34). San Francisco: Jossey-Bass.

Fullan, M. (1986). *Performance appraisal and curriculum implementation research*. Manuscript for the Conference on Performance Appraisal for Effective Schooling, Ontario Institute for Studies in Education, Toronto, February, 1986.

Fullan, M. (1991). *The new meaning of educational change* (2nd ed.). New York: Teachers College.

Fullan, M. (2001). *The new meaning of educational change* (3rd ed.). New York: Teachers College.

Gallagher, K. S. (1992). *Shaping school policy: Guide to choices, politics, and community relations*. Newbury Park, CA: Corwin.

Guba, E. G. (1984). The effect of definition of "policy" on the nature and outcomes of policy analysis. *Educational Leadership, 42*(2), 63–70.

Heck, R. H. (2004). *Studying educational and social policy: Theoretical concepts and research methods*. Mahwah, NJ: Lawrence Erlbaum Associates.

Hill, M. (1997). *The policy process in the modern state*. Hemel Hempstead, UK: Prentice Hall.

Hjern, B. (1982). Implementation research: The link gone missing. *Journal of Public Policy, 2*(3), 301–308. https://doi.org/10.1017/S0143814X00001975

Hogwood, B., & Gunn, L. (1997). Why 'perfect implementation' is unattainable. In M. J. Hill (Ed.), *The policy process: A reader* (2nd ed.) (pp. 217–225). London: Harvester Wheatsheaf.

Imber, M. (2001). The struggle for equity. *American School Board Journal, 188*(8), 33–35.

Ingram, H. (1977). Policy implementation through bargaining: The case of federal grants-in-aid. *Public Policy, 25*(4), 499–526.

Knott, J., & Wildavsky, A. (1991). If dissemination is the solution, what is the problem? In D. S. Anderson & B. J. Biddle (Eds.), *Knowledge for policy: Improving education through research* (pp. 214–224). Bristol, PA: Falmer.

Koenig, L. W. (1986). *An introduction to public policy.* Englewood Cliffs, NJ: Prentice-Hall.

LaRocque, L. (1983). *Policy implementation in a school district.* (Unpublished doctoral dissertation). Simon Fraser University, Vancouver, BC.

Levin, B. (2004). Making research matter more. *Education Policy Analysis Archives, 12*(56). 1–20.

Levin, B., & Young, J. (1994). *Understanding Canadian schools: An introduction to educational administration.* Toronto, ON: Harcourt Brace.

Levin, B., & Young, J. (1998). *Understanding Canadian schools: An introduction to educational administration* (2nd ed.). Toronto, ON: Harcourt Brace.

Lindblom, C. E. (1959). The science of muddling through. *Public Administration Review, 19*(2), 79–88. https://doi.org/10.2307/973677

Lindblom, C. E., & Cohen, D. (1979). *Usable knowledge: Social science and social problem solving.* New Haven, CT: Yale University Press.

Loveless, T. (1998). The use and misuse of research in educational reform. In D. Ravitch (Ed.), *Brookings papers on education policy* (pp. 279–317). Washington, DC: The Brookings Institution.

Majone, G., & Wildavsky, A. (1977). Implementation as evolution. *Policy Studies Review Annual, 2,* 103–117.

Marshall, C., & Gerstl-Pepin, C. (2005). *Reframing educational politics for social justice.* Boston: Pearson.

Marshall, C., Mitchell, D., & Wirt, F. (1989). *Culture and education policy in the American states.* Philadelphia: Falmer.

McDonnell, L. M., & Elmore, R. F. (1991). Getting the job done: Alternative policy instruments. In A. R. Odden (Ed.), *Education policy implementation* (pp. 157–183). Albany, NY: State University of New York.

McLaughlin, M. W. (1987). Learning from experience: Lessons from policy implementation. *Educational Evaluation and Policy Analysis, 9*(2), 171–178. https://doi.org/10.3102/01623737009002171

McLaughlin, M. W. (1991). The Rand change agent study: Ten years later. In A. R. Odden (Ed.), *Education policy implementation* (pp. 143–155). Albany, NY: State University of New York.

McLaughlin, M. W. (1998). Listening and learning from the field: Tales of policy implementation and situated practice. In A. Hargreaves, A. Lieberman, M. Fullan, & D. Hopkins (Eds.), *International handbook of educational change* (pp. 70–84). Dordrecht, The Netherlands: Kluwer. https://doi.org/10.1007/978-94-011-4944-0_4.

McLaughlin, M. W., & Pfeifer, R. S. (1988). *Teacher evaluation: Learning for improvement and accountability.* New York: Teachers College.

Montjoy, R. S., & O'Toole, L. J. (1979). Toward a theory of policy implementation: An organizational perspective. *Public Administration Review, 39*(5), 465–476. https://doi.org/10.2307/3109921

Musella, D. F. (1989). Problems in policy implementation. In M. Holmes, K. A. Leithwood, & D. F. Musella (Eds.), *Educational policy for effective schools* (pp. 96–97). Toronto: OISE.

Nagel, S. S. (1980). The policy studies perspective. *Public Administration Review, 40*(4), 391–396. https://doi.org/10.2307/3110267

O'Day, J. A., & Smith, M. S. (1993). Systemic reform and educational opportunity. In S. H. Fuhrman (Ed.), *Designing coherent educational policy: Improving the system* (pp. 250–312). San Francisco: Jossey-Bass.

Odden, A. (1991). *The evolution of education policy implementation.* Albany, NY: State University of New York.

O'Reilly, R. R. (1991). Educational policy research in Canada. In R. R. O'Reilly & C. J. Lautar (Eds.), *Policy research and development in Canadian education* (pp. 1–5). Calgary, AB: University of Calgary.

Owens, R. G. (1998). *Organizational behavior in education.* Needham Heights, MA: Allyn and Bacon.

Ozga, J. (2000). *Policy research in educational settings.* Philadelphia: Open University.

Pal, L. A. (1987). *Public policy analysis: An introduction.* Toronto: Methuen.

Pal, L. A. (1992). *Public policy analysis: An introduction* (2nd ed.). Scarborough, ON: Nelson Thomson Learning.

Pal, L. A. (1997). *Beyond policy analysis: Public issue management in turbulent times.* Scarborough, ON: ITP Nelson.

Pressman, J. I., & Wildavsky, A. (1973). *Implementation.* Berkeley, CA: University of California.

Principles. (1992). *Webster illustrated contemporary dictionary.* Chicago: Ferguson.

Prunty, J. (1985). Signposts for a critical educational policy analysis. *Australian Journal of Education, 29*(2), 133–140. https://doi.org/10.1177/000494418502900205

Quade, E. S. (1975). *Analysis for public decisions.* New York: American Elsevier.

Rich, J. M. (1974). *New directions in educational policy.* Lincoln, NE: Professional Educators.

Rideout, D. (1995). School councils in Canada: A cross-country survey. *Education Canada, 35*(2), 12–18.

Ripley, R. B., & Franklin, G. A. (1982). *Bureaucracy and policy implementation.* Homewood, IL: Dorsey.

Sabatier, P. (1993). Top-down and bottom-up approaches to implementation research. In M. Hill (Ed.), *The policy process: A reader* (pp. 266–293). Hemel Hempstead, UK: Harvester Wheatsheaf.

Sabatier, P., & Mazmanian, D. (1980). The implementation of public policy: A framework of analysis. *Policy Studies Journal: the Journal of the Policy Studies Organization, 8*(4), 538–560. https://doi.org/10.1111/j.1541-0072.1980.tb01266.x

Sandell, S. (1977). Does your board need its own policy analyst? *American School Board Journal, 10,* 48–49.

Scheirer, M. A., & Griffith, J. (1990). Studying micro-implementation empirically: Lessons and dilemmas. In D. J. Palumbo & D. J. Calista (Eds.), *Implementation and the policy process: Opening up the black box* (pp. 163–179). Westport, CT: Greenwood.

Sergiovanni, T. J., Burlingame, M., Coombs, F. S., & Thurston, P. W. (1992). *Educational governance and administration* (3rd ed.). Needham Heights, MA: Allyn & Bacon.

Sergiovanni, T. J., Burlingame, M., Coombs, F. S., & Thurston, P. W. (1999). *Educational governance and administration* (4th ed.). Needham Heights, MA: Allyn & Bacon.

Silver, H. (1995). Policy problems in time. In E. W. Ricker & B. A. Wood (Eds.), *Historical perspectives on educational policy in Canada: Issues, debates and case studies* (pp. 30–40). Toronto: Canadian Scholars' Press.

Simon, H. A. (1957). *Administrative behavior.* New York: Macmillan.

Taylor, S., Rizvi, E., Lingard, B., & Henry, M. (1997). *Educational policy and the politics of change.* New York: Macmillan.

Thompson, J. T. (1976). *Policymaking in American public education.* Englewood Cliffs, NJ: Prentice Hall.

Values. (1992). *Webster illustrated contemporary dictionary.* Chicago: Ferguson.

Weatherley, R., & Lipsky, M. (1977). Street-level bureaucrats and institutional innovation: Implementing special education reform. *Harvard Educational Review, 47*(2), 171–197. https://doi.org/10.17763/haer.47.2.v870r1v16786270x

Weiss, C. (1982). Policy research in the context of diffuse decision making. *Journal of Higher Education, 53*(6), 619–639. https://doi.org/10.2307/1981522

Weiss, C. (1991). Knowledge creep and decision accretion. In D. Anderson & B. Biddle (Eds.), *Knowledge for policy: Improving education through research* (pp. 183–192). London: Falmer.

Wildavsky, A. (1979). *Speaking truth to power: The art and craft of policy analysis.* Boston: Little, Brown and Company. https://doi.org/10.1007/978-1-349-04955-4.

Wildavsky, A. (1985). The once and future school of public policy. *Public Interest, 79*(Spring), 25–41.

Williams, W. (1982). *Studying implementation: Methodological and administrative issues.* Chatham, NJ: Chatham House.

Wirt, F. M., & Kirst, M. W. (1992). *Schools in conflict.* Berkeley, CA: McCutchan.

Wu, X., Ramesh, M., Howlett, M., & Fritzen, S. (2010). *The public policy primer: Managing the policy process.* London: Routledge.

Zald, M. N., & Jacobs, J. (1978). Compliance/incentive classifications of organizations: Underlying dimensions. *Administration & Society, 9*(4), 403–424. https://doi.org/10.1177/009539977800900401

About the Author

Jerome G. Delaney is currently Associate Professor of Educational Administration in the Faculty of Education at Memorial University of Newfoundland. He holds undergraduate and graduate degrees from Memorial University and a Ph.D. in Educational Administration from the University of Alberta. Prior to his entrance into academia, he was a high school teacher in the Newfoundland public school system and went on to serve as principal in three high schools in the province. Jerome teaches undergraduate courses in effective teaching, educational administration, and education law, and graduate courses in education policy and law, administrative theory and practice, and leadership theory and practice. His primary research areas are education policy, education law, and effective teaching. He welcomes feedback at jdelaney@mun.ca

Subject and Name Index

A

administrative operability, 12
administrative procedures, 65
Alexander, 27
Australian classification, 16

B

Ball, 26
Berliner, 67, 71
Bosetti, 80
Boyd, 2, 70
Braybrooke, 77
Brown, 32, 33
Burlingame, 3, 42, 54, 74, 77

C

Caldwell, 3, 80, 81
Canady, 3
capacity building, 21, 22
Carley, 36
choice (value in policy), 9
Cibulka, 95
Clear And Simple Analysis (CASA),
    29, 30, 31, 32
Clemmer, 14, 19, 20, 21, 22, 36, 37,
    38, 39, 54, 55, 56, 59, 62, 63,
    64, 73
Clune, 67, 80, 96
Cohen, 69, 70, 85
Colebatch, 26, 43, 52
computer technology, 64
consequential policies, 14
Coombs, 3, 42, 54, 74, 77, 93, 94, 95
Cunningham, 3

D

Darling-Hammond, 86, 87
de facto policies, 15
definitive policies, 20, 21
Delaney, 89, 90, 91, 92
delegated policies, 15
deregulatory approach to policy, 18
descriptive analysis of policy, 28
distributive policies, 16
Downey, 3, 24, 25, 45, 46, 50, 51, 52
Duke, 3

E

education policy
    defined, 3, 4
    significance, 1
education reform, 84, 85, 86, 87
educational research, 67, 68, 69, 70,
    71, 72
effect category (of policies), 19
effective implementation guidelines,
    50, 51
effective policies criteria, 54, 55
efficiency (value in policy), 9
elitist approach to policy, 7
Elmore, 21, 46, 47
equity (value in policy), 9, 79
evaluation analysis of policy, 28
evaluation studies, types of, 56, 57, 58

F

Facebook, 81
Fairclough, 82
feminist approach to policy, 8

Finn, 68
First, 3, 39, 40, 41, 65
formal policies, 15
Fowler, 4, 10, 52
Franklin, 47
Fritzen, 81, 82
Fuhrman, 95, 96, 99
Fullan, 46,78, 98

G
Gallagher, 11, 24, 29, 30, 31, 32
Garet, 69
Gerstl-Pepin, 4, 16, 81
Griffith, 59, 60
Guba, 4
Gunn, 47, 48, 49

H
Heck, 70
Henry, 7, 16, 17, 18, 26, 36, 37, 42, 79, 84, 86, 99
Hill, 77
Hjern, 44
Hogwood, 47, 48, 49
Howlett, 81, 82

I
Imber, 79
incremental approach to policy, 18
inducements, 21
Ingram, 47
Internet, 64

J
Jacobs, 46

K
Kirst, 74
Knott, 60
Koenig, 42, 53, 56, 57, 58

L
LaRocque, 44
legal rights, 1
Levin, 4, 71, 74, 75, 76
liability, 93
Lindblom, 70, 77

Lingard, 7, 16, 17, 18, 26, 36, 37, 42, 79, 84, 86, 99
Lipsky, 46
Loveless, 68

M
macro-macho approach, 2
Majone, 46, 47
mandates, 21
Marshall, 4, 8, 16, 81
material policies, 17
Mazmanian, 44, 47
McDonnell, 21
McDonnell and Elmore classification of policies, 21
McLaughlin, 46, 47, 84, 85, 99
micro-incremental approach, 2
Mitchell, 8
Montjoy, 46
Musella, 44, 45

N
Nagel, 1
neo-marxist approach to policy, 7
Newfoundland and Labrador Safe and Caring Schools Policy, 17
nonrestrictive policies, 20

O
O'Day, 85
Odden, 21
O'Reilly, 69
O'Toole, 46
Owens, 76
Ozga, 69, 70

P
Pal, 8, 25, 28, 29, 34, 35, 43, 52, 52
Pfeifer, 46
Plank, 2
pluralist approach to policy, 7
policy analysis, 2
  defined, 24, 25, 26, 27
  forms, 27, 28, 29
  models, 29
  tips for good, 34, 35

policy benefits, 5
policy coherence, 95
policy development, 36, 37, 38, 39,
    40, 41
  approaches, 37, 38, 39
  cycle, 39, 40
  elements of, 36, 37
policy dissemination, 39, 59, 60, 61
  defined, 59, 60
policy evaluation
  defined, 52
policy implementation
  approaches, 43, 44, 45
  assumptions, 45, 46
  defined, 42, 43
  research findings, 46, 47
policy manual, 64, 65
policy rage, 1, 93
policy websites, 64
political viability, 11
prescriptive policies, 20
Pressman, 48
principles
  defined, 10, 11
procedural approach to policy, 18
process analysis of policy, 28
Prunty, 7

Q
Quade, 25, 26
quality (value in policy), 9

R
Ramesh, 81, 82
rational approach to policy, 18
Realistic Model for Policy Analysis,
    32, 33
redistributive policies, 16
regulations, 63
regulatory approach to policy, 18
restrictive policies, 19
Rich, 60
Rideout, 74
Ripley, 47
Rizvi, 7, 16, 17, 18, 26, 36, 37, 42, 79,
    84, 86, 99

S
Sabatier, 44, 47
Sandell, 25
Scheirer, 59, 60
Sergiovanni, 3, 42, 54, 74, 77
Silver, 1, 93
Simon, 77
Smith, 85
social media, 60
Spillane, 85
Spinks, 3, 80, 81
symbolic policies, 17
system changing, 21, 22

T
Taylor, 7, 16, 17, 18, 26, 36, 37, 42, 79,
    84, 86, 99
Thompson, 78
Thurston, 3, 42, 54, 74, 77
Twitter, 81

V
values
  defined, 10
values in policy, 7, 8, 9, 10

W
Weatherley, 46
Webster, 10
Weiss, 70
Wildavsky, 2, 27, 46, 47, 48, 60
Williams, 25
Wirt, 8, 74
Wu, 81, 82

Y
Young, 4, 74, 75, 76

Z
Zald, 46